HOT MAN

Music in American Life

A list of volumes in the series
Music in American Life appears at the end of this book.

HOT MAN

The Life of Art Hodes

Art Hodes and
Chadwick Hansen

Discography by
Howard Rye

University of Illinois Press
Urbana and Chicago

© 1992 by the Board of Trustees of the University of Illinois
Discography © 1992 by Howard Rye
Manufactured in the United States of America
C 5 4 3 2 1

This book is printed on acid-free paper.

Library of Congress Cataloging-in-Publication Data

Hodes, Art, 1904–
    Hot man : the life of Art Hodes / Art Hodes and Chadwick Hansen.
        p. cm. — (Music in American life)
    Discography: p.
    Includes bibliographical references and index.
    ISBN 0-252-01753-6 (acid-free paper)
    1. Hodes, Art, 1904–   . 2. Jazz musicians—United States—
Biography. I. Hansen, Chadwick, 1926–   . II. Title.
III. Series.
ML417.H72A3 1992
786.2′165′092—dc20
    [B]   90-19876
                                                                CIP
                                                                MN

This book is a blues for all the musicians and the music we have lost, but the authors want to make personal dedications as well. Art Hodes's part is for his mother, Dorothy, and his wife, Jan. Chad Hansen's part is for his brother Alan.

Contents

Illustrations follow page 50

Preface

Art Hodes is one of the last survivors of the generation of white jazz musicians who learned their trade in Chicago in the twenties. His career has been long and distinguished. The list of musicians he has played with reads like a jazz hall of fame; it includes Louis Armstrong, Bix Beiderbecke, Sidney Bechet, Barney Bigard, Frank Teschemacher, Pee Wee Russell, Jack Teagarden, George Brunis, Eddie Condon, Pops Foster, Milt Hinton, George Wettling, Kaiser Marshall, Baby Dodds, Chippie Hill, Mama Yancey, and so many more that it would be virtually impossible to name them all. He has played most of the major jazz clubs in New York and Chicago, the two cities that, after the decline of New Orleans, have been the centers of the music, and he has recorded prolifically. He was virtually a staff pianist for Blue Note in the forties, when that company was establishing itself as one of the major jazz labels, and he has recorded for literally dozens of others.

Art has always been very much his own man, musically as well as personally, and therefore he doesn't fit easily into any of the usual categories. His roots are partly in the Chicago style, except that his playing is blacker than that of most of the white Chicagoans. His strongest roots are in the blues. One critic remarked as early as 1939 that he was the only white pianist who could play the blues convincingly, and many others have echoed that judgment since.

He is also one of the few jazz musicians who has worked hard at educating the public about the music. In the forties he did a jazz show for WNYC, New York's public radio station, and, in the late sixties and early seventies, a series for educational television. In the forties he was coeditor of *The Jazz Record*, a little magazine that is still a mine of information on the music and the musicians. He has lectured and played at dozens of colleges and universities, and at high schools as well. Most important, he has also reached the public through his writings, in little magazines, in *down beat*, and in general circulation magazines and newspapers.

Some years ago Art and I published an anthology drawn from the pages of *The Jazz Record,* which we called *Selections from the Gutter* (Berkeley: University of California Press, 1977). The first section was made up of sketches by Art, which, as I pointed out in introducing them, provided "a brief but impressive autobiography, full of the people, the places, and the music that made up one musician's life." Shortly thereafter we began talking about the possibility of doing a full-scale autobiography.

We knew from the beginning that it would not be the usual as-told-to life, in which the musician talks into a tape recorder and his collaborator edits the tapes into a coherent narrative. We wanted to start with Art's writings. There were a lot of them, both published and unpublished, all of article length.

Art writes well. He is a gifted storyteller, with a voice as unique and authoritative as his piano style, but he writes anecdotally rather than historically. One incident or person or place will remind him of another, and associations of this sort frequently replace narrative. We needed a narrative structure and we needed transitions to organize and make sense of the anecdotes, and we discovered after a series of attempts that Art was not going to provide them. It was partly that he tended to think anecdotally, but there were other difficulties as well. The largest of these was that Art is a modest and private person, in spite of having spent so many years in the public spotlight. There are some things he cannot or will not say, but which needed to be said.

A further problem was that Art, like all gifted storytellers, has frequently told the same story several times over in different contexts. Very occasionally there would be contradictions in fact between one version and another, usually caused by the lapses in memory that happen to anyone who is recalling events that happened twenty, or thirty, or even sixty or more years ago. These were easily caught and corrected. The larger problem was that details of the same story varied in emphasis and effectiveness from one version to another, and it was clear that each story could be made more effective by combining the strengths of several different versions.

We agreed, then, that while the raw materials would be Art's, I would do the editing and provide the transitions and the background and commentary needed to put the book together. I had several kinds of raw material to work with. The largest and most useful body of published writing had been written for *The Jazz Record* from 1943 through 1947. Then there was the column—"Sittin' In"—that appeared in *down beat* throughout the sixties. There were articles and interviews in many places, both little magazines and general circulation magazines and newspapers. And there was an even larger body of unpublished writings, ranging in length from two pages of typescript to twenty-five.

Then there were tapes: four reels of Art's playing and talking, mostly about his years in New York, recorded by Dr. Harry van Velser, and four cassettes of questions by me and answers by Art, made to fill in gaps in the narrative. Finally, there were my own memories. I got to know Art first in 1950, when I was a graduate student at the University of Minnesota, and running a jazz record shop as well. So I've heard Art tell many of the stories in this book many times over, and when I remembered a particularly vivid phrase—for example, Art's saying that when Pee Wee Russell played "High Society" "it came out 'Low Society' "—I didn't hesitate to use it.

A few of the stories in this book are based primarily on a single written or taped source, but most of them are composites. In constructing a typical incident I've used from four to six sources: some written, some taped, some remembered. It has been the most time-consuming writing I've ever done, a process not unlike the making of commercial recordings, in which you take two bars from this version, then two bars from that (after correcting a clinker with a tiny splice from version one), then four bars from a third version, and so on. When I have used copyrighted material I have been careful to stay within the bounds of fair use, but Art and I would like to thank the editors of *down beat* for their permission to use materials from his column, "Sittin' In." The account of buying a Leroy Carr record in Chapter 5 is based on a *down beat* column of April 12, 1962. The description of the Dodds brothers' band at the end of Chapter 5 is based primarily on columns of June 8, 1961, and September 13, 1962, and the account of playing with Bob Scobey in Chapter 13 is based on a column of December 5, 1963. Many phrases and some sentences from other *down beat* columns are scattered throughout.

The reader should be warned, then, that although when Art is speaking the words are always his, the sentence structure is often mine and the larger narrative structure is always mine. I have tried, however, not to get in the way of his voice. Art once said about his piano playing that he was "part schooled and part primitive," and the same might be said of his language. Both the music and the language have rich rewards for the attentive listener. The music is suffused with the blues, and in many ways this book is itself a blues—a lament for and a celebration of a music that has been here and gone.

In the following chapters my words are set in italic type in order to distinguish them visually from Art's words. The reader should also know that when the words "Negro" and "colored" are used rather than "black" or "African American" it is because that particular passage was originally published at a time when those were the polite words for African Americans.

I want to thank Judith McCulloh, executive editor, and Rita D. Disroe, manuscript editor, of the University of Illinois Press for editorial assistance that has been sympathetic and supportive as well as thoroughly professional.

Chadwick Hansen

1

The Rainbow Gardens, I

Jazz, especially the blues, has been Art Hodes's life. Whitney Balliett said of him in a New Yorker *review that he "is probably—though he is rarely given his due—the greatest of blues pianists." He learned his trade in Chicago in the twenties.*

Back then, says Art, "They didn't call you a jazz man, they called you a hot man." You supplied the heat—that special intensity with which a single musician can bring an otherwise dull band to life, and bring an audience to life as well. But before he was a jazz musician he was a popular musician. He learned music—and the music business— before he learned jazz, and he got much of his education on his first full-time job, at the Rainbow Gardens Cafe on West Madison Street in Chicago. The owner, the man who hired him, was one of Al Capone's gambling bosses, Dago Lawrence Mangano.

I remember auditioning for the job. Madison at Laflin isn't exactly what you'd call a plush neighborhood, nor was it then, in the early twenties. The derelicts and bums had taken over Madison Street; this was their home. From Canal Street on west to Halsted it was thick with end-of-the-liners. Both sides of the street featured bars where cheap whiskey and wine headlined the menu. Flophouses, cheap hotels, beaneries, Army and Navy stores, cheap picture shows, drunks, drunks, drunks. Fights a daily routine. The Black Maria stops to carry out a stiff. The Salvation Army band trying to save a soul. The guy lying on the street, out of his mind. You walk around him. Women to match, the bottom of the heap.

It thins out a bit as you walk west. At Laflin we're getting into the rooming-house district. The Rainbow Gardens occupied space over a store on the southwest corner. Don't ask me how it got its name; I never saw a rainbow in the joint. Anyway, you climbed twenty-five stairs—I counted them many times—and there you were, into a small dining room. I'd guess you could seat fifty adults. White tablecloths, waiters in tuxedos, several entertainers (female, of course), and the large upright piano. There was a kitchen, and the food, Italian style, was good. Entertainment started at 9 P.M. and continued till 4 A.M.

So late one afternoon there I was, playing for the Dago. I don't remember what I played, but I got the job. Mangano knew and liked music. He had two brothers who were professional musicians. Lawrence played an expensive banjo, tuned ukulele style, and played and sang songs mother never taught me. His favorite tune was "It's Tight Like That," and I, who have heard thousands of verses, still remember one of his—unfit to print. As I remember it, after I'd played a bit the Dago got out his banjo and I accompanied him.

My boss was one of Chicago's tough men. He was a big man in his way. He never spent much time in the joint, but left the running of it to his woman, Lucy Labriola. She was my direct boss, and she treated me OK. For that matter, so did he, but he had other businesses. I heard rumors of this and that but all I actually knew about was his gambling house. I had the bad sense to try out the poker game once—and just once.

Lucy was a big round woman: pleasant, bustling, active. I can't remember anything bad about her, certainly nothing evil. The Dago was built along similar lines, not quite as tall, five feet ten I'd guess. Looked powerful and weighed around the two hundred mark.

One experience there stands out vividly in my memory. Two young chaps, about twenty-five or so, came in one night and started picking up drinks at other people's tables and taking them away, claiming they were federal agents. One was acting up; the other fellow was just with him. Someone phoned the Dago and in less than ten minutes he was there, he and a few of his boys. By that time there were just a few customers left, and they were shooed out and the door was locked. The boss went to work on this "agent," who of course turned out to be a phoney. Well, that's the first time I ever saw someone worked on.

The boss got him in a corner. "So you're a federal man? Let's see your badge." And as the guy reached for his pocket Mangano kicked him in the shins. When he doubled up he got hit in the stomach. Same routine: first the question, then the kick, then the stomach or the face. It went on longer than I could stand. Nobody interfered. This poor guy's companion just got tagged a few times for being in bad company. The bad actor was thrown down the twenty-five stairs; the other guy got shoved down. The front door was opened. Someone pulled the first guy out, grabbing him inside his coat collar, dumping him in the alley. It was quick, fast, efficient. The front door remained open, the boys left, and we were back in business. I never saw either of those guys again. Nor did I hear of any police investigation. Nothing.

And how about the time we were all leaving the Rainbow Gardens, 4 A.M., when three hoods jumped the boss. He fought them single-handed all over the sidewalk until they beat it, one by one. And when someone asked him why he didn't use his gun the Dago said, "Waste lead on them punks?"

The Rainbow Gardens bought its liquor from the Genna Brothers gang and one night they paid the place a visit in force.

Eighteen of them marched up those stairs. Lucy had tears in her eyes. She had to serve them, and it was common gossip that that gang had taken care of her husband. It was just a sample of their sense of humor, being served by the woman who had cause to hate you.

Well, here they were, seated right smack at the piano, the favorite son, Angelo, at the head of the table right next to me. I recognized at least one guy I'd grown up with. Nervous? But I kept playing. Pretty soon the drinks arrived. They spotted me almost immediately as being green, and someone decided I should have a drink. I mean I got a drink from everyone at that table. It was put right on top of my piano. More humor. You know up until then I'd never messed with it, didn't like the smell. And now eighteen shots to down. I did, but you talk about a sick boy. For the next six months you couldn't pay me to take a drink.

Gangster humor as Art knew it was always rough but not always that vicious. The black porter at the Rainbow Gardens

was very religious, carried a small Bible with him, and when he'd get egged on he'd preach to the Dago to repent. There was the time the Dago sent him out to get small change for the register; when he came back the Dago goosed him. Man, there were dimes and nickels flying all over the place.

But the Dago was good to Art, even protective, as he was when Art slapped a singer who had cheated him out of his fair share of a tip.

It was a good-looking entertainer. I saw her get a two-dollar tip, and I watched her hand me fifty cents. I was fit to be tied. Words flew out of me and then my hand reached out and slapped her across the mouth and I walked out of the place. Sure, I was green—never heard the show must go on. I just figured that's that and I'm through. I stayed away two days; then the Dago called me. By this time I understood enough to know that when the Dago called, you showed up. He got me in the kitchen. I never forgot his lecture. "Listen, kid, don't ever slap anyone here. If something happens that you don't like, see me, but don't ever do that again." I didn't. Much later I found out that this particular chick was a gangster's gal. The Dago had given her a job as a favor. I could have gotten myself into a mess of trouble.

When Mangano was shot twenty years later, in 1944, Art read about it in a New York newspaper.

No doubt the Dago had it coming. The law of the mob seems to be kill or be killed, and fifty-four is a long time to live if you're a gangster. They put two hundred shotgun slugs in him and five bullets, and he lived seven and a half hours. After they'd pumped lead into him once he got out of his car and started after them, pure instinct, but they weren't taking any chances. They circled the block and came back to finish up. They did. Of course I was sad when I read it.

And he was sad when he read ten years later that the body of Paul "Needlenose" Labriola—Lucy's son and Mangano's stepson—had been found stuffed in the trunk of a car with that of another gangster. Art remembered him as a seven-year-old in a military school uniform,

a small chubby lad, healthy looking. Poor Lucy. She'd lost her husband, a court bailiff, in '21, a gang killing. Then the Dago got chopped down. A few years pass and her brother Paul Rossi gets the same treatment. And now it's her own boy. How many times I'd seen them all at the Rainbow Gardens.

Art liked Lucy, and he liked the Dago, and he had to admire his courage.

You don't forget the Dago's guts. Pure guts. The time the Captain's house was bombed the Dago was picked up for questioning and they held him for one week. He sure looked a mess when he got out, but the word was he didn't talk.

But he doesn't like to remember the other gangsters he has known. If you press him he will volunteer that he knew Machine Gun Jack McGurn, the man who planned the St. Valentine's Day Massacre, but it is clear that he doesn't understand the fascination gangsters have for people who have had no experience of them. He once said of his good friend Pee Wee Russell that Pee Wee was "one of the gentle people." So is Art, and part of his gentleness is an acquired taste.

Chicago taught me long ago not to look around too much. Go to work, do your job, have your fun, but be careful not to pick on the boss's girl, or girls of his close friends, friends of his friends, relatives, or even a fifth cousin of his mother-in-law. You just didn't do that. I did it once, but I always had to learn the hard way.

2

Growing Up

Art Hodes was born in Nikolaev, Russia, on November 14, 1904. The date, like all of the dates in his early life, might be off by a year or even two. His parents didn't keep records, so he depends on family traditions and memories. When he was six months old the family came to America, to New York City. Of New York, Art says,

I recall next to nothing, yet we were there till about the time I was six years old. What I do remember is my mother telling me how I would react when my dad took off for work. "You would chase your father down the street, begging him not to go."

When they moved to Chicago they settled in a third-floor cold-water flat at 1243 W. 12th Street (now Roosevelt Road) in what was then Chicago's ghetto, in the "Bloody Twentieth" Ward. The neighborhood was changing; Jews were moving west and Italians were moving in. But the Hodes family weren't movers, so when the city widened 12th Street and their building had to be torn down, they moved just a few blocks away to another third-floor cold-water flat at 1039 S. Racine Avenue. The building is still there today.

They got along well with their neighbors.

Pop didn't scare easy so folks let him be. Mom was the mixer and had a heart of gold. She had nothing but friends no matter what nationality. Everybody knew her, and if she could do you a good turn she would. So it was friendly in that building.

But out on the streets it was different.

The city streets were the playgrounds and you could grow up rough. The area was heavily Italian. Anyone of a different nationality stood out like a sore thumb and was fair game. It was a job trying to go to school. I can't recall how many times I was cornered by more than one lad. Sometimes I even got away, but there was one time I didn't. It was after a summer-school class. The teacher would walk us out as far as she could before turning off to go her way. That's when a group attacked us and before I could get away I was hit over the head with a sandbag. I felt that for weeks.

When the family first moved to Chicago they bought a piano on the installment plan, but when Art's father temporarily lost his job it had to go back. They didn't get another until they moved to Racine Avenue, when Art was eleven. By that time Art's mother had discovered Hull House, the famous Chicago settlement house founded by Jane Addams, and he took music lessons there from 1916 to 1920. His teachers were the Smith sisters: Gertrude, who taught piano, and Eleanor, who taught voice.

At Hull House, if you studied piano you had to take voice. The singing class was free, and the piano lesson was the huge sum of twenty-five cents.

At the time he resented the voice lessons.

I had to be enrolled in a choir full of girls; I was the only boy in the room. I could hear the boys outside playing ball. But what it did for me musically I can never overappreciate. Each week I was put into a different section, so I sang soprano parts, alto parts, tenor, bass. I grew to hear all the different parts. I developed my ear. And oh how that helped me when I began to hear music I liked and was able to pick it up and play it by ear.

But there was much more to Hull House. There was the summer camp that I could get away to for two weeks, somewhere near Waukegan. So much to do at Hull House. You could play basketball, go to gym, or theater. Occasionally I'd pass Jane Addams. I can still remember the sight of her; in a way she reminded me of my mother, sort of short, buxom, filled out, grey hair and the warmest eyes. This woman had taken a part of a city block and carved out a bit of humane living for I don't know how many thousands of kids.

And I'll never forget that sign as you entered the theater. It was just above the door, and it read, "Act Well Your Part; There All Honor Lies."

The piano playing taught at Hull House, of course, was standard

*piano-teacher fare: semiclassical and some classical. And there was music
around the house. Art's father had studied voice in Russia.*

He would have loved to become a singer. He had a good voice, but
in Russia it took more than a good voice. Pa's professor took him
aside one day and asked him, "William, what do you do for a living?"
Pa told him, "I'm a tinsmith; I work with a hammer." To which the
prof replied, "Take that hammer and knock any ideas you have about
being a professional singer out of your head."

But Pa had his Caruso records, and Chaliapin, and in between he
would raise his voice in song. Usually he'd sing Russian folk songs.

My older sister, Sema, was the first to take piano, and she got
interested in popular sheet music. I could pick up the tune just by
hearing her practice; I'd really play at it. Pa wasn't much for that sound,
so I did my thing during the day. He liked to hear me play Chopin,
and some of Chopin I really dug. One short thing he wrote I've promised
myself I'd record some day. It had all the depth of a blues I could
work on.

But what really got me turned on to pop music was radio, that little
crystal set. You could hold one in the palm of your hand. I remember
evenings where I sat glued to that set. I went to sleep with it in my
ear. At best what I heard was pseudo-jazz, the Coon–Sanders Night-
hawk Orchestra out of Kansas City. I was a fascinated listener and I
could pick up tunes by hearing them. In the daytime I'd be at the
piano, trying them out. In those days, if a player could do that well
he'd be known as a good faker.

*Art played pop music with a strong beat, and when they discovered
that at Hull House they enlisted him to play for dancing classes on
Saturday afternoons. One afternoon the dancing master asked Art if
he'd mind if someone played clarinet with him.*

So the band director brought this young kid up on the stand. The
biggest thing about him was his head, the physical size of it. I remember
he was very sure of himself as he put his clarinet together. When he
played I could see why. He got around on his instrument.

*The young clarinetist's name turned out to be Benny Goodman. The
Goodman family lived further out on the West Side, and they, like the
Hodes family, had discovered Hull House. The two would play together
only twice, and they were to move in very different directions musically,*

Goodman eventually going to big-band jazz, Hodes staying almost re-
ligiously with small bands.
    Art's mother, Dorothy,

had a dream that I'd become a great pianist.

But his father, because of his own experience in Russia, couldn't imagine
one of his children becoming a musician.

Pa had it figured out that both of my sisters, Sema and Zena, would
become schoolteachers and that I would be a civil engineer.

So Art, who had done well in grade school, was sent to a technical high
school, Crane High School.

He couldn't see that I didn't have my head screwed on that way and
I couldn't tell him.
    In the beginning it wasn't too bad. I got interested in wood work,
and in foundry I came up with interesting results. But somewhere along
the line I began to have dizzy spells; I'd have to hold onto a railing
to keep from tumbling downstairs. And there was no use talking about
it at home, not when I couldn't put it into words. It was while this
was hitting me that I discovered algebra wasn't for me. And it was at
this time that I met my first Negro. He wasn't a musician, not that I
know of, and he too wasn't an algebra freak. Our teacher was handing
out report cards. "Hawkins and Hodes," he called out. We came to
the front of the room. Then in a loud voice—I can still hear him—
he said, "Hawkins and Hodes, if I was going on a fishing trip I couldn't
think of two better lads to take along. But in algebra?" And he handed
us our report cards. We'd both flunked.
    That's where it began. I started to ditch school, and I discovered
Chicago's Loop. Especially I discovered a burlesque house. It was at
State, possibly at the corner of Van Buren. If you got in in the mornings
the fee was a quarter, exactly my allowance to get to school, get a
bite, and get home.

So he spent his school hours at the burlesque house, or in one of the
other Loop theaters, and among other things he heard a lot more music,

usually a small group, the drummer with his gadgets to emphasize some
bit that was happening on stage. I caught Clayton, Jackson, and Durante; they sang "I Wonder What Would William Tell When He Came
Home to Ma."

Eventually, of course, the school sent a report card home, saying he had been absent, and his father issued an ultimatum:

"If you're not going to school you're going to work." And I chose work. I didn't know what I was getting into. I had no abilities, just youth. I wasn't organized; I wasn't disciplined. I took all sorts of jobs, most of them unpleasant. I never lasted too long. Messenger boy, delivery boy, parcels, storerooms. Even tried a sweet shop. There I learned how kids stayed away from eating what's behind the counter. No one said don't, so you did. So you got sick, real sick. I worked at a can-making company. All I picked up there was the smoking habit. I was in and out of work so fast it would make your head swim.

Coming into September my older sister said to me, "If you'll go back to high school and finish I'll buy you a fountain pen." And I didn't have to go to a tech school. Believe me, that sounded good to me. I enrolled at Medill High School and made it right on through. I graduated.

At that high school the kids discovered that I could play piano and they enlisted me to play during breaks in classes. I was popular, sought after, and I liked it. I didn't know it then but I was getting a workout. I was learning, getting relaxed playing for listeners and watchers, and improving right along. Going to school I was going to school. It would stand me in good stead.

He had begun gigging—playing occasional jobs for pay.

During the time I was day-jobbing I got acquainted with the kid across the street. Barney was Italian, about my age, and played drums. He had neighborhood connections. If there was an Italian wedding coming up he'd know about it and many a time come up with the gig. People could afford five bucks apiece pay to a couple of kids where they'd shy off of hiring pros. So many a weekend I'd be with Barney, playing in some hall. Some weekends we'd have two jobs, Saturday and Sunday. And I was getting exposure; other musicians were hearing of me. I started getting calls. And I'd play dime-a-dance halls. I had a lot of spirit in my playing, and the guys alongside me enjoyed it, and that made me enjoy it even more. I didn't know it but I was getting hooked for music.

Art had played a few gigs with a drummer named Freddie Janis, and shortly after he graduated from high school, Janis gave him a call. Would he like to audition for a steady job playing piano? It payed thirty-five dollars a week to start. When he had worked his series of day jobs

I never made over seventeen bucks a week and never liked any of 'em. Oh boy, would I audition. So late one afternoon there I was, playing for the Dago.

3

The Rainbow Gardens, II

"OK. Start next week. Thirty-five bucks." The boss had taken a liking to my playing and besides he was saving fifteen a week by hiring me. Later I was told more about the job.

"You start at nine and you go to four. You play for two singers and in between you keep the piano going. You get half the tips the girls make." The Dago knew that I was green and never played for singers, but he told me to take my time and keep trying and I'd learn. "And if they squawk we'll fire 'em and get some others." He kept his word, because they sure did some squawkin'. Hell, I could only play in the key of C, F, and G. Flats and sharps scared me. What stood me in good stead was the ear training I got at Hull House. I could fake. Let me hear a tune a couple of times and I could play it in any key I knew. What I had to learn was more keys, and I had plenty of time to learn in.

Some of the gals were real kind and patient to me. The first few months it couldn't have been easy for them with my lack of knowledge. A few just quit because I couldn't play in their keys. Some got fired. But I kept on experimenting. Little by little I learned to play in a few more keys and added numbers by memory. I stayed there eighteen months in all, and before I left that job I was known in the trade as a good entertainer's piano player.

It wasn't a long walk to work from my house. Nine on the button I'd hit. Usually I'd play a few tunes, like "Running Wild," "Somebody Stole My Gal," "Frivolous Sal." Then I'd vamp a few bars of a tune that one of the entertainers used a lot. That was her cue to get up from wherever she was sitting and wander over to the piano and tell me what number she wanted to sing. Usually she'd warble one chorus from beside the piano and then she'd make the rounds, go from table to table. Sometimes I'd get a fast cue to go into something else that a customer requested. I'd have to keep my eyes open. At the end of her turn she'd come back and stuff whatever she got into my pocket. Each gal used one of my pockets to stuff the tips in. And brother, there was no fooling about tips. Never nothin' but green.

They used to enjoy crying-in-your-beer tunes. "The Ace in the Hole" was always a tip tune. A good entertainer, with her heart in her song, never missed. By the end of my first week I was rich. Can you picture a lad not quite twenty earning around a hundred bucks a week? That was me. Bank your salary, pay your way at home, and walk around with plenty scratch in your pocket. I mean, tips were good. Pop didn't know what to make of it.

But I earned it. I sat at that piano from 9 P.M. to 4 A.M. A couple of times during the night I could sneak out to the boys' room. Not too often. And don't think I'd get lost in there, 'cause the knock came and the voice rang out, "There's a lull in the joint." I believe that's one sentence I grew to hate.

The piano player had to keep the lull out of the joint. When it starts getting quiet in a cafe people get restless and leave. That's bad. So I learned to play without killing myself, and when a live one came in, a man with money, we all came to life. Song after song for him; the gals would come up and stuff the money in my pocket. A bartender once told me, "I can do more tricks with this towel"—the wet towel he used to wipe the bar. He was explaining how loose change left laying on the bar, preferably by a drunk, could disappear. Well, those chicks I played for got the same effect with a handkerchief, and most of 'em carried one in their hands as they sang. At the Rainbow job I never used my salary. I bought a car, nice clothes, and was in the chips.

And so I got a bit calloused. I watched people get drunk. I saw a lot of night life. I got better acquainted with the piano. Singers began to like my playing. I got a bit relaxed. I began to look around, visited other joints, met the help. Musically that place was swell for me. I learned lots of tunes, I developed my ear. It got so all a gal had to do was sing the melody to me once or twice and away we went. That was wonderful training. I began to hear harmonies I never knew existed. Before I left I was getting offers right and left to work other places.

Over the next twelve years or so Art would work at dozens of places around Chicago, so many that he hasn't any clear idea how many. But some of them stand out. For instance, there was the time he was working for the Dago once more, but at another place.

This was maybe a couple of years later, a New Year's Eve, the dead of winter. Man, it used to get awfully cold in Chicago. And boy, you sure could freeze in that town. This was Halsted Street, where Blue Island Avenue runs into Harrison. Somewhere in that neighborhood Mangano operated a night club. Tonight it was full, people getting drunk and celebrating. Upstairs, unknown to the customers (many of them), was a gambling joint. You could lose plenty up there. Johnny Craig, a drummer, and I were playing downstairs, "I've Grown So Lonesome Thinking of You," when suddenly we weren't lonesome any more. Pop! Pop!—the Fourth of July, pistols and all. And me with my back turned. Man, I was scared. I ducked. Some joker celebrating, shooting at the ceiling, and it was made of tin. Those gamblers upstairs must have done some moving around.

Well, this celebrator couldn't have shot all his bullets away when the Dago came out of the kitchen, fit to be tied, picked up a heavy old-fashioned water pitcher, walked up to this guy with the gun in his hand, and stretched him cold with one blow on the top of his skull. And if it hadn't been for his woman pleading with the Dago and getting in his way, Lawrence would have kicked and beat him to pieces, he was that mad.

After it was all over, two dicks—plain-clothes men—came in, walked straight into the kitchen, stayed there about ten minutes, and then walked out into the night. Later I found out it had cost the boss fifty bucks apiece to keep it quiet.

Art also worked in less dangerous places.

Cafes in those days were about all alike. If it was a real class spot it sported a five-piece band and an intermission piano player and singers. A floor show would consist of an MC, a line of girls, the singers in the place. The band was strictly for background and a little dancing. Not much dancing—a boss can't make money with you out on the floor, away from the table. The entertainers were the most important people in the place. The band was at the bottom of the ladder. The piano player was more important; we had our social status, you know. The first few days in a new place you'd feel like you weren't wanted. Everyone put on airs. If you were still there a week later you'd fall in place.

The first real band I heard was in a high-class cafe on Wabash Avenue. [Up to that time he had been working in places that had only a pianist, or piano and drums, or at best a trio: tenor-sax, piano, and drums.] A friend of mine, a drummer named Harry Smith, had the band, and Joe Sullivan was playing piano in that band. I'd got a job playing for entertainers there. The band was getting sixty bucks a week; I was getting twenty-five. But when I took the job the boss told me, "If you make less than a hundred at any time, quit." I stayed there for several months and the first time I made less than a hundred dollars I quit. I used that as an excuse because I liked to move around and by then I was in demand.

I remember Sullivan and I having an argument because I played on the piano he used. He told me, "You're an entertainer's piano player. Lay off my piano." At that time Joe was listening to Earl Hines at the Apex Club, but I'd never heard a colored man play.

4

Learning Jazz: Delavan Lake

In the early eighties Art was playing solo piano three nights a week in the Lobby Lounge of the Mayfair-Regent, a very plush hotel at the south end of Chicago's Gold Coast. It is in many ways a pleasant room, but the carpet is so thick and soft that when Art tried to tap his foot it only sank into it. So he took to bringing a thin board to work which he would place under the piano. Against it his foot could mark and feel the beat over which all of his improvisations are constructed.

As long as he can remember, Art has had a good beat. That is why he knows there was also a carpet on his first job, at the Rainbow Gardens. It can't have been as thick or as soft as the one at the Mayfair-Regent, but there has to have been a carpet, because Art formed the habit of tapping his foot against the side of the piano to keep the beat.

Mangano noticed. He told me, "You either stop kickin' my piano or I'll tie your foot." That's something I never got over, I mean to this day. As well as I can recollect my main thing was swing—the left hand [with which he also marks the beat when he is playing in a band. He is what used to be known in the trade as a two-fisted pianist.] The main thing I had to learn was the style, the idiom, which the blacks had and I didn't.

Art had been raised only about four miles from 35th and State, which was then the jazz capital not only of Chicago's black belt but also of the world. But

I'd never been out to the South Side. You stayed in your own neighborhood pretty much.

So like most young white musicians in the twenties he heard his first jazz on phonograph records, and he didn't hear it in Chicago.

I met Earl Murphy, who was then playing banjo, and when some drummer Murph knew was looking for a piano player who would go out of town on a summer-resort job, Murph recommended me, and I went.

The drummer's name was Les; he was the leader. Les was crazy about the way I played waltzes, and he also liked my natural way of swinging. The other men, besides Murph, Les, and myself, played violin, sax, and trumpet. They were all better "paper" men than I was; all had more [musical] schooling.

The place where we worked, Delavan Gardens, was about two city blocks, at the most, from a beautiful lake. The working hours were short, the pay was good. Delavan Lake. Get up in the morning, go down to the lake, row, swim (I mean try), loaf around. That's where I was introduced to jazz—to Armstrong, Dodds, Ory, Bix—a new world for me—through Murphy's record collection.

Almost immediately Murph got on me to listen to his Louis records and the way the rhythm played behind Louis. And he played Bix records. In a short while I'd bought some records of my own, and a victrola, and I was studying jazz intensively. When I first heard the Hot Five records, Louis knocked me out—his ideas, his thoughts—while the rest of the band didn't penetrate my skull. In fact for a long time I couldn't understand Kid Ory, or that style of playing. It seemed rough and a bit harsh to me. Then I only had ears for Louis. And Bix, I liked him immediately, but I could feel that he didn't have the rhythm behind him that Louis did. Many were the discussions we had then as to who was greater, Louis or Bix.

And from then on I always had trouble of one sort or another with the men I worked with, first on that job and later on others. You see, in the Hot Fives that Louis made, he didn't use drums, and the piano, Miss Lil, and the banjo, St. Cyr, had to carry the beat. The result was that Miss Lil had to play a lot of left-hand chords, "solid" piano, instead of spreading out. Without thinking about this at the time I started pounding out chords, which knocked the drummer, Les, out of his mind. And many were the arguments that followed. One time I even got invited outside. But I kept playing that piano my way, except on those waltzes. We played plenty of those.

The dance hall could hold a thousand people and on Saturdays did. That's when we'd have to "pep it up." That was the expression then. "Tiger Rag" was the order of the day, up tempo, everybody on his feet. We had a character on sax by the name of Baker who could do less moving around than anyone I ever saw. He'd cross his feet, put his sax on one side, and play. Saturday night, with the place going like mad, Baker would sit there and hardly move. Les, sitting behind him, would reach over with his drumstick and clip him sharply on the dome, hoping to get him to come to life and stand up and let it out. Not Baker. He'd uncross his feet slowly, and turn around slowly and look at Les, and turn back slowly and resume playing his way. Yes, Les had troubles with the band that summer—on top of living with his wife's family.

Lots of things happened to me on that job. Did you ever hear of a Dr. Clark who wrote a book called *How to Live and Eat for Health?* Somehow or other Murph and I discovered him. I think the violinist put us on his track. Anyway, it says in the book that meat and potatoes don't go together—drink 'steen glasses of water daily—eat this—don't eat that. We started getting particular about what we were fed, stuck up our noses, so to speak, and more troubles appeared on this peaceful summer resort job. One thing, Murph and I were in the best of possible health. That was the healthiest period I can remember.

Sometime during the summer two young chaps (one an athlete) who "knew Tesch" [the great jazz clarinetist] came over to our place and we got acquainted. They were staying a few miles away. They knew the language so well, and knew all the boys I'd heard of but never met, that in no time I was hanging on their every word. It seemed we were friends.

Seemed is right. On a July 3rd evening they invited the band to their cottage. Nobody accepted but me. We listened to records and made plans for the next day. On the fourth we got up and went out. They both had pistols, and I watched them shoot at targets. I wondered at the time about the guns, but didn't question them. I had to play a doubleheader, two sessions, the fourth, so they drove me back early.

The boys grabbed me when I got back. "Boy, wait till you see your room—man, oh, man!" Someone had robbed me of everything I had. That was one bum kick. And I had to work through that day. Someone told me about the company I was keeping, but I stoutly defended them. Yes, and they kept running around with me all the following week. Helped pick new clothes for me. Sometime later, after they had left, we read about them in the papers. They'd driven to some town and held up a shoeshine shop. A colored boy working there grabbed one of their guns and shot one of the two, killed him. He was the one I liked most. The other got away but was caught and sentenced to forty-odd years. Funny thing, they had two guns. One they forgot to reload. Probably since the fourth.

It seemed I was always running into characters. Instead of meeting the right people and doing the right things, I'd get mixed up with the wrong people, and do the wrong things. Instead of taking the "Twilight in Turkey" route, it had to be "Gut Bucket" and "Yes, I'm in the Barrel."

Well, I was so brought down by all this that I took to gambling with the natives and some of the boys in the band. And luck stood alongside of me all summer; I just couldn't lose. It was fifty one night, eighty the next. The boys got disgusted. They tried everything; they even threw a "special" party for me on my last night there. I won that night too. I bought new clothes, records, and came home with a pocket full of dough.

That job ended in an awful hurry for me. One day at dinner someone put one of those advertisements of "I used to be skinny like you but look at me now" under my plate. Well, I blew my top and walked out. So the leader came over to give me my notice. I guess I felt the same way he did, because I quit on the spot. They got Dave Rose to follow me in—*the* Dave Rose. I went back to Chi.

That was, Art thinks, the summer of 1927. Art was twenty-two, and when he got back to Chicago his education in jazz was to begin in earnest.

Like all of the major jazz musicians, Art has a style that is his and no one else's. If you listen to him with any care, you'll know him the next time you hear him. How he developed that style is something he can't describe or define, except to say that it's his way of speaking the musical language of jazz, of telling his own story. That is not to say that it is entirely devoid of influence, as some jazz musicians pretend of their own styles. One can hear something of Lil Hardin in the way he drives a band with his left hand, something of Earl Hines in an occasional right-hand phrase, and something of the many pianists he followed on Chicago's South Side in the blues that suffuse much of his playing. But the style as a whole is unique.

Like all individual styles, however, it is part of the more general style that is the musical language of jazz, and nobody has spoken more acutely of how he learned that language than Art Hodes.

5

Learning Jazz: The South Side

It was after I returned from Delavan Lake that I had my first encounter in person with the great Negro musicians. I was to become very well acquainted with Louis Armstrong, and to see quite a lot, and what was more important, hear a lot, of Earl Hines. I was to become friends with Zutty Singleton. Let me tell you about the Wingy Manone days.

I was introduced to him at our union in Chicago. I'd made friends with a lot of musicians who congregated at the union hall three or more nights a week. There were at least three pool tables and sometimes as many as thirty card games going on at the old union, and leaders hired their men there. There was a real good feeling in that place, although at times the boys got to arguing a bit. Well, I fell right in and was doing all right at about the time someone introduced me to Wingy. He immediately started talking big about who he was and what he'd done. I was very much unimpressed and left him with one of those "glad to have met you" routines that people go through with. But we met again.

This time he was looking for a pianist, and Ray Biondi [the guitarist] was trying to help him find one. They finally fell into where I was working. They stood in the basement underneath the band and listened, and Ray tells me that when Wingy heard me play he said, "That's the man I want."

And so started a most important period in my life. In a short time we were roommates, then buddies, the best and closest of friends. We lived every minute of each day, and each day was a complete life in itself. Wingy and I moved in together first at a Near-North-Side hotel, where we did it up right. Wingy would get on the phone and call all over the country. The Ford had to be washed, greased and delivered.

We ate the best. Louis Armstrong was at the Savoy, playing in Carroll Dickerson's band, and we were steady customers. We lasted two weeks at that hotel and they wound up holding our bags.

And then we moved to the North Side proper, Lawrence Avenue, around some kids from New Orleans that Wingy knew, and in no time at all, I knew. And the tales I heard from them about New Orleans, and Mardi Gras, and the musicians! In me they had a real listener. Anybody from New Orleans had a beat, could feel the music. I'd been led into a completely new world than the other I'd known at the union floor.

Wingy owned a victrola and a half-dozen records, all by Louis, which he played and replayed. Anybody who was somebody stopped at our apartment at some time. The list would sound like a *Who's Who* in jazz. The main reason, the only one, was Wingy — his personality. He was a funny man and good kicks were plentiful around him.

In the two years I lived with Wingy I don't believe I read one book. Our day was so packed with listening to music and playing music and going to see people from our world, mainly Louis Armstrong, that we had no time for reading. We didn't miss it; we didn't know books existed.

Each day was about the same, except for the people we'd run into. Wingy had such personality, could be so funny, and above all could really play then. He had a beat you couldn't get away from. If we had two blocks to walk, we'd walk it in time. Wingy would sing some song as we walked along and we'd both swing along in time. Those couple of years I lived with Wingy, we lived with a beat. Our mistress was music; we worshipped her as a god. From the morning when we'd start in on the vic till late at night when we were exhausted and had to go to sleep, we had but one desire — to play, to play better this minute than we had the last, or to hear something played that would knock us out. I'd wake up with Louis's "Muskrat Ramble" on the vic, and immediately I was back in time, walking to the music, dressing to it, and being walked out of the house.

We didn't see people who would break the spell. Out to the Savoy Ballroom to hear Louis. At that time Louis Armstrong could have been elected Mayor of the South Side; he was loved. I can still see him being carried clear across the dance floor of that huge Savoy Ballroom by his cheering fans. Tell me, when's the last time you saw a jazz musician carried on the shoulders of his fans? When Louis picked up his trumpet and blew he was "callin' his children home." That man could blow no wrong. And what a warm person to be around.

The joint was always packed and it would take us minutes to get to the back where the bandstand was. But Louis would see us at once, and his face would light up and we'd feel warm inside. And right after the set we'd go back with the band into the band room. We hung out there like groupies. Most likely Joe Oliver—King—would come in for his visit and there'd be a lot of good feeling in the room. And somebody would say something funny, and that would give Louis an opening and you couldn't beat Louis at being funny—not even Wingy. And we'd laugh through the whole intermission, and then slowly walk Louis back to the stand. And then we'd wait for the band to begin playing again, and for it to be Louis's turn to play. Man, the guy could really blow then. How we wanted to be in the same league. Not the formula, just the feeling. To be able to say the same things, just for the pleasure of saying them.

Wingy had a big bear coat that we took turns wearing. Louis used to greet us with "Who's the bear tonight?" The boys in the band kept a flat especially for themselves, to be able to drop in at all hours and relax. You know the conversation that takes place on the record "Monday Date" where Louis says to Earl Hines, "I bet if you had a half pint of Mrs. Circha's gin . . ." (and I'm spelling her name the way it sounds; I've never seen it in print). Well, that was the name of the woman who kept the flat for the boys. For a half-buck you got a cream pitcher full of gin, which was passed around as far as it would go. In those days that was what the boys drank.

Louis, knowing I loved blues, took me and Wingy to a barbecue place on State Street near 48th where the primitives, the pianists that came up from the South, hung out. They'd fall in there looking for a bite to eat, or a buck to pick up, because they had a kitty there, and if you played you'd pick up something. That's when my real jazz education started. The place itself was a wooden shack, badly in need of repairs, really not much to look at, but to me it couldn't look better. It was everything I could wish for. That place and its people taught me about the blues.

After that first time Wingy and I went there with our gang—Krupa, Freeman, Tesch, and the rest. Wingy didn't go that much. He was a trumpet player, and what a trumpet player wanted to hear was Louis. But I never lost the habit of going there. Often I'd go there alone.

One night on entering the barbecue I heard a three-piece band playing: sax, piano, and drums. I got acquainted immediately. That rhythm impelled me to say hello. The drummer's name was Papa Couch. I forget the sax player's name. The piano player was Jackson.

A few days after I'd met him I happened to hear him playing alone and I was startled. He could really play the blues—they flowed out without an effort. I can't begin to tell you what that sound did to me. This was the first time I had heard the blues really being played. I found out later on that he'd just been released from a hospital. Been laying there with a broken leg, thinking about that wife of his who'd left him. When he got out he had the blues. He was really down. When he sat down at the piano those notes would tell all that.

Art followed many pianists on the South Side. Little Brother Montgomery said to him a few years before he died, "You know you used to follow me." But it was Jackson who taught him the most.

I followed Jackson for days. After a while I noticed that he wasn't playing the blues so much. He bought a new suit; I met his new girl. Soon he stopped playing the blues altogether. He would play popular music. Well, I played popular music better than he did, so I would ask him to play the blues. Finally he said to me, "Man, what you always asking me to play the blues; you know, I ain't got the blues." That's how I learned the blues was more than music.

There were no schools where one could go and learn to play jazz. These people were my teachers. I went among them, lived with them, absorbed their music, and came away enriched. Every night that I was free and had some money I'd go down to the barbecue joint, eat, and then sit around putting my nickels into the player piano, with the rolls that were made by black musicians. They also had a juke box of sorts, which had records by pianists who were blues pianists—Hersal Thomas, Pine Top Smith. I heard those people on that juke box, and they were tremendous, and this was the real fine blues of that time. And of course I heard Leroy Carr.

The part about the barbecue place that was so tremendous was that it exposed you to a bit of the life that these people lived. I mean after they got used to you, so you was part of the furniture. They knew you were there but they could still act themselves. I still recall the time I came in there alone and about a dozen colored folks were sitting and singing and I sat down and they kept on singing and I felt good, and it sounded good. I came to be accepted by these people as one of them, and believe me I never abused the privilege. I never messed with their women. I was just plain music hungry.

There was a grandfather there, or a very elderly guy who had to carry a cane to walk, and he would do a dance with that cane and knock you out. The music would get going and he'd get up there and do this little shuffle thing, and somebody would drum and somebody would sing, and all this would go on any one evening that you were there listening.

Many times they'd ask me to play. I was kidded plenty. Someone would holler, "Play the blues, Art," and when I played they would laugh. Not mean, but they would laugh. That hurt, but I couldn't blame them. I hadn't as yet learned the idiom. I was entranced by their language but I hadn't learned to speak it. The next night I was there again, putting my nickels into that piano. That music did something to me I can't explain. I had to hear it. That's one feeling that never left me. Jackson would say to me, "Art, I'll show you how to play the blues; just watch my hands." And I'd answer him, "No, don't teach me, just play." Because I knew I couldn't learn that way. I knew that I had to feel the blues myself and then they'd flow easily.

Eventually, of course, people stopped laughing. Art remembers especially a time when he visited Jackson

at a cabaret on West Division Street. After climbing about twenty-five stairs and knocking on a door, an eye would peer out at you from behind a peephole. If you looked OK you got in. Jackson got me in the first time. After that they knew me. Inside was a lunch counter, farther on a gambling room, with the piano going. Jackson insisted that I play the piano. Well, the crap game was making a lot of noise, but some time after I started playing it got quiet. Those gamblers had stopped playing and were listening. Man, it's like no other feeling I can describe. Everyone with you, and you're it. It was like graduating. Jackson took me home with him and I lived at his house for days.

Most of us Chicago lads learned from the great Negro players who went there from New Orleans and elsewhere. They inspired us; we came, we listened, we learned. If piano was your instrument you dug Earl Hines or Teddy Weatherford. Trumpet? Louis Armstrong. Clarinetists followed Johnny Dodds or Jimmy Noone. Drummers paid extra attention to Baby Dodds.

So it went, with most of us not only falling in love with the music but with the Race too. You could get lost out on the South Side. It was a new world, with so much to see and oh, so much to hear. I heard more music then by accident than I do today on purpose. Just walking down a street early in the morning, and hearing some brother whistle a greeting to another on his way to work.

I would bring two or three people at a time to the barbecue place. I brought Benny Moylan; he played sax. I brought Johnny Lane; he played clarinet. Two fine white pianists came later, George Zack and the late Frank Melrose. I don't know how many others they brought. It became a place to go, a hangout.

A couple of doors from the barbecue was a storefront church, a black church. And many times as you walked by you would hear them having religion, and the beat going on, and the after beat. People singing—shouting. A church with that sound coming out of it. Right across the street was a flat, and the drummer lived there, Papa Couch. Papa and Mama Couch. I don't know how schooled he was. I know he owned a set of drums, and I know I liked the way he played. It was a simple style, not far removed from those small bands that played for nickels and dimes and quarters anywhere on the streets of Chicago. Sometimes you'd catch them on the bridge on Michigan Avenue, just by the river. You'd catch these little bands playing, you know, with a washtub [bass].

Papa Couch had a player piano, and you could drink gin, which was illegal, of course, and smoke tea. That's another high that came from New Orleans. So many times we'd go across the street. Dave Tough came along one night. Dave was a little under the weather, and he needed help. And the squad car happened to go by and saw a black and a white helping a white across the street, and that looked suspicious. So they followed us into the apartment moments later and arrested everybody because they were drinking gin.

The police put them all in a cell together until court opened in the morning. Tesch's wife was along that night. Art doesn't remember who else, except that there was a group of them. They didn't have a bad night of it; they talked and smoked their tea. In those days the police didn't recognize the smell of marijuana, because so few people smoked it.

Next day I heard a judge dismiss us by saying, "Why don't you stay in your own neighborhood?" And of course if everybody stayed in their own neighborhood there'd be no enrichment. What if Columbus had stayed in his own neighborhood?

On the South Side the music was everywhere:

It's summer, 1929, 35th and State, a record shop. The turntable spins and the music is being heard outside: the curb is occupied with listeners. It's the same record being played over and over. I ask the clerk, "Ma'am, what is that?"

"That's Leroy Carr; it's "That's All Right for You, Baby." I must have a copy, and she sells me the only one she has, the one spinning on the turntable. As I leave, the curb listeners disperse. That record has been like medicine to me at times. It's a bit of greatness. He played himself inside of me.

Or there was the time Art was walking the South Side, "probably high."

It was dead of winter. Cold, man, like it only can get cold, icy, in dear old Chi. Not that it made any difference. I still made my merry way, looking, seeking out all the colored music I could find. Night time, of course; whoever went looking for it in the day? So I found myself alone, walking the streets of the South Side. Just to hear a colored man whistling a blues paid off. Not like today, with some Tin Pan Alley tune coming from the lips. No, man, this was still the real thing. But look here; isn't that Stepin Fetchit advertised at this theater? Darned if it ain't. But that below it; man, I'm in luck today. If I ain't dreaming that's Bessie Smith. Let's go.

Inside, it was the picture that was on. Not a damn thing about it I can remember. All I know is I waited it out. There it goes, finished. And now the orchestra climbs into the pit, the overture, and that was a honey; and there's Stepin Fetchit. There's a guy that surprised me. I'd always pictured him as a guy that moves slower than slow. That was his Hollywood character. This must be a different guy. Funny? He had me roaring. But I was in for a treat. Evidently I had caught the first show of the week. The band and the actor weren't exactly together, but Mr. S. sure straightened that out in a hurry. Talk about a guy doing his act and rehearsing the band at the same time, this guy was it. How he improvised. Instead of blowing his top when the music went wrong, he called loudly for a phone and the prop man brought it out. He got on the phone and called—guess who?—the orchestra leader, and in a sweet professional way, yet never losing his audience, he straightened him out on what had to be, and what wasn't. It was my first and most impressive lesson in stagecraft. And that audience was right with him; they didn't miss a trick. It was sure something to hear.

Now comes the big hush. Just the piano going. It's the blues. Something tightens up in me. Man, what will she look like? I ain't ever seen her before.

Now I hear her voice and I know this is it . . . my lucky day. I'm hearing the best and I'm seeing her, too. There she is. Resplendent is the word, the only one that can describe her. Of course, she ain't beautiful, although she is to me. A white, shimmering evening gown, a great big woman, and she completely dominates the stage and the whole house when she sings "The Yellow Dog Blues." Ah! I don't know, she just reaches out and grabs and holds me. There's no explaining her singing, her voice. She don't need a mike; she don't use one. Everybody can hear her. This gal sings from the heart. She never lets me get away from her once. As she sings, she walks slowly around the stage, her head sort of bowed. From where I'm sitting I'm not sure she even has her eyes open. On and on, number after number, the same hush, the great performance, the deafening applause. We won't let her stop. What a woman. If she has any faults, like the big head, the prima donna, it doesn't seep through. You just don't get that feeling from her. You just know you're listening to the greatest blues singer you've ever heard.

Outside it's still cold. I don't know when I get up to go and I'm sure I'm not sure where I'm going; just walking. But there's a record playing back something that was recorded, recorded in my head. There's that one woman's voice, "Oh, you easy rider, why don't you hurry back home. . . ." So help me, I still hear it.

Besides Louis Armstrong, besides Jackson, besides Bessie Smith, there was Earl Hines, whom Art used to hear at the Grand Terrace. "The first time I heard Earl Hines," says Art, "it made me want to take my hands and throw them in the lake." And there was the Dodds brothers' band (Johnny on clarinet and Baby on drums; both former members of the King Oliver band), who impressed Art most for their tight ensemble, so different from "the players that only hear themselves. When their chorus is over, the music has ceased. Like the guy who's thinking about what he's going to say while you're talking." The Dodds brothers played at a club on the Near North Side, Kelly's Stables. It was a two-story building. Nothing on the first floor but a cleaned-out stable. You went upstairs to a big room (I'd guess two hundred people could get in). Red table cloths, no decor, swinging waiters who sang on occasion. Plus music. When you walked in, you pulsated. Every number was an entity. Yet you were recognized as you came in their club. They smiled, nodded, but it kept coming out so good. A six-piece band, stretched straight across the bandstand, the drums at one end, the piano at the other, in between absolute togetherness. Everybody listening to each other. What one played was important to the other.

I think we were all listening, and to the same thing. I'm still listening, and I'm still hearing it. It's part of me, as if we were married. I hear what's going on today. You play the blues well in any language and I'll like it. You don't have to wear a 1920s costume to catch my eye. But to begin with, I do have a music. I have a heritage. This isn't just something that can come unglued from a sheet of music. This is something that goes on inside of me.

And you want to know if I still practice? That's the least I can do for what I've gotten. As my doctor once told me, "I haven't arrived; I practice medicine." Me too. I haven't arrived. Just making the trip daily.

6

Hot Man, I

Besides introducing Art to the South Side, Wingy also introduced him to the small, intense world of the white jazz musician.

Every hot man looked up to Wingy. He lived the music. Our apartment was like a *Who's Who*: Max Kaminsky, Alvin, Krupa, Teschemacher, McKenzie, Wettling, Paul Mares. For me it was all school, only school was never like this. You awoke to music, and you were swinging all day. At night it was for real—the jam session, sitting in. I don't know how many piano players I gave free lessons to. Walk in on their job and ask to sit in. They not only got a rest, they got a lesson.

The other side of the intensity, however, was economic insecurity, the price the jazz musician paid for his kicks, because even in the Jazz Age jazz was less popular than popular music, or than jazz-tinged popular music. Remember that it was Paul Whiteman who was called the "King of Jazz," not Louis Armstrong. And if the title had still been around in the fifties, one can be sure it would have gone to Stan Kenton rather than Charlie Parker. And besides the problem of popular taste, the very intensity with which the hot men lived made for anything but security.

Shortly after Art and Wingy met they recorded together, on December 17, 1928: two sides for Vocalion, "Trying to Stop My Crying" and "Isn't There a Little Love?" At this writing they're still available in the MCA Jazz Heritage series, in an album called "The Chicagoans." It started with a club date.

Augie Schellange, the New Orleans drummer, had gotten a job at a place on North Clark Street, the Breakfast Club. Later it became the Liberty Inn. Augie called Wingy, so Wingy and I went to work there, also Boyce and Harvey Brown—five pieces. Harvey played guitar, Boyce alto sax. We enjoyed playing together, but it only lasted a short time.

The fourth night on the job, about one hour after we'd come to work, Augie gets off the stand and starts packing up his drums, very quietly, without talking to anyone, with plenty of people in the place. No one wanted to ask Augie questions. He looked, and acted, and talked tough, and we just didn't want to bother him with questions. When he got all packed he walked over to the boss and asked for his pay, and what was more, got it.

We were mystified, and it took us a while to find out what was wrong. Well, Boyce and Harvey were both interested in Yoga and Hindu philosophy; in fact quite a few of the leading hot musicians in Chicago had gotten interested in it, and there was lots of discussion going on. Boyce and Harvey had talked about Yoga on the job, and Augie was a low-down, gut-bucket drummer who'd happened to wander into a conversation between the two brothers and didn't like all the talking that was going on.

The guy could drum, and he loved to drum. When Wingy got the date with Vocalion, Augie was tending bar at a Capone joint on the South Side. He had his set of drums set up there, and there was a piano, and that's where we rehearsed for the date. Even before that we'd played there—Wingy, Wade Foster on clarinet, Augie, and I. At that time I still had much of my original style of playing. I'd only heard two pianists on records, the only two pianists to that date who had made any impression on my style of playing, Hines and Miss Lil Armstrong. I'd fallen right in with Augie, and also with Wingy. Neither of them ever criticized me at any time. I remember asking Wingy at the record date how I should play when Tesch took his chorus, and Wingy answering, "Play like you always play."

Well, there at Augie's bar we'd play music together with no listeners but ourselves, and when it got good you'd probably see Wingy walking around patting the wall, and just Wade, Augie, and me playing, and then just Augie and me, and nobody saying a word. Didn't want to break the spell. But when it did break they'd come back in, and we'd play a few choruses and take it out. And then we'd sit around happylike and kid among ourselves.

Those were the days. The last thing we talked of was getting paid for playing. We wanted a job so we could keep playing together. Yeah, that didn't last long. Four days work, a few rehearsals and a few nights playing for our kicks, and a record date, and so long Augie.

The date was a windy one. Wingy picked me up in his car. Away we went to Augie's place, where the rest of the gang was—Tesch, Snurps, Augie, and Ray Biondi. We sat down and started playing, playing just anything. When the band really started sounding right, Wingy broke it up and away we went to the studio.

After the engineers had padded the bass drum with everything in sight, and after they had seated us just the way we wouldn't seat ourselves if we had anything to say about it, we started in. We fluffed very few sides. I think Wingy cleared his throat on one take. Anyway, that was that.

My first out-of-work experience came after I discovered jazz. With the discovery came a change of style, and I became less popular with leaders. And the crash hurt everybody. During the period with Wingy, he would want me to be at liberty so that we could play together, so outside of the one time of dire necessity—the hotel was holding our bags—when he allowed me to go to Colosimo's for two weeks, I don't recall working if it wasn't working with him. I'll always remember Wingy answering the phone one day. "Hello. . . . No, this isn't Art. . . . Yes, Art's working—with me. . . . Yes, I'll tell him you called." And I was standing right there, and we could have used that money. We were both low. But we wanted to stick together and play together, and nothing else was more important to us then. If we weren't working we were out of work, and we just played for kicks. And somehow we ate.

After a couple of years Art and Wingy split up, but there were still good times together. Art remembers especially one all-night session:

"Bix is in the house."

The word had passed all around and the next any of us knew a spotlight played on his table and finally found him, and it continued to glare on Bix till he consented to play, although it took a good deal of applauding. He was there to get his kicks, not to sit in. But the public (and the house that night was almost all musicians) were not to be denied. Bix got up and wandered over to the bandstand.

The place was My Cellar, on State near Lake Street. Sam Beers owned that joint. Wingy had the band, and I wasn't in it. In fact we weren't speaking at the moment. I forget just why. But when Bix got up to play, Wingy came over to me and asked me to sit in. Wingy's piano player just didn't know the tunes.

So I sat in with Bix, and we jammed. There was never a lull that night; we played on into the dawn. Sterling Bose relieved Bix, and Wingy played some. I got up from the piano when Bix felt like noodling. Bob Conselman played drums. At 6 A.M., when the porter started sweeping up around us, we knew it was time to break up. Bix was still blowing, and me too. I hated to go home.

That was in 1930, and by then Art was "scuffling, doing all kinds of jobs." In 1931 he worked at a taxi-dance hall,

the Capitol Dancing School, Randolph and State, 4th floor. Tony de Lancey was the boss, a well-bred college man, and he knew how to pack the place. He had the prettiest chicks in Chi working for him. Bud Freeman had the band there before I got the job. Dave Tough was on drums; Tut Soper was his pianist. For some reason the boss got himself sold on me and gave me the job.

Opening night he presented me with a basket of flowers that topped me in height, and then made a speech about his new band. What an opening. I had a four-piece band: LeRoy Smith on clarinet, Earl Wiley on drums, and Earl Murphy on banjo and guitar. The joint was jammed. The boss bought us a gallon of wine and that set the pace from then on in. We got so fixed that first night that Murph finally broke all his banjo strings trying to play as loud as the rest of us and had to play his guitar. He hated that, 'cause in that quartet you couldn't hear it. All of a sudden, from behind me, I heard what sounded like a pistol shot. So did the boss. Out he ran from his office with his two pearl-handled revolvers unholstered, ready. And what do we see? Murphy holding his guitar, its neck broken, dangling. He'd gotten so mad at the damn thing that he busted it on the piano bench. We calmed him down, brought him into the office and set the jug by his side, and played out the night with three pieces.

I'll always remember the music we played. We didn't bother to learn the pop tunes of the day, and we didn't play any tunes we thought weren't any good. We developed a set of deaf ears [to requests]; this was one joint where the customer was never right. Certain originals I've recorded for Blue Note were part of our nightly repertoire, also such tunes as "Dr. Jazz," "Shoe Shiner's Drag," "Kansas City Stomp," "King Porter Stomp," "I'm Gonna Gitcha," and "Original Dixieland One-Step." The funny thing about this is that the joint remained packed every night, and people danced, actually danced to jazz and liked it.

Le Roy played a cornet style on his clarinet. Wingy Manone dropped in on us, listened to the band, then said, "Hell, you guys don't need a trumpet." And that rhythm section really moved along. Dave Tough was another constant visitor.

That was an exciting job for Murph. He was attractive to women, and in that joint he could pitch a ball. He did. But it wasn't long before some customer got peeved at him over some chick. It got back to Earl that this guy was out to get him, so Murph took to wearing a gun. We kidded him about it: "At a time when all the gangsters are ditching their rods you go to carrying one." Then one night his pistol fell out of his pocket and someone told the cops. The next I knew Tony de Lancey said to me, "Just got a call from the station; Murph's been picked up with a rod." We rushed over and Tony used his influence. He had enough in his pocket to choke a horse. Murph was back on the stand the next night, owing the boss his life.

After we'd been on the job a while Le Roy decided to leave and we got Benny Moylan to join the group, the man with that wonderful voice and own style of tenor playing. It was about that time that the boss decided to spread out and go into the night club business. That was the beginning of the end. He started pouring his winnings into his losings and it wasn't long before we were behind in our pay, way behind. Came the day that we all decided this couldn't go on any longer; something had to be done. But what? We finally hit on a solution. Saturday night, when the joint filled up with customers, I was to call the boss up at the Kentucky Club (that was the name of his ill-fated nitery) and tell him to instruct the cashier to give us some back salary or else — or else we'd quit right then and there. Boy, did you ever hear a telephone rattling? This one did. He blew his top. He talked to me, argued, cajoled; finally threatened me with a ride. I stuck to my guns, but so did he. His answer was "No dough." Well, no doughee, no playee.

Up to that stand I marched, told the fellows to pack up on the double (and they didn't waste a second), and got Wiley to give me a roll on his drums. The astonished customers gathered around me as I announced our withdrawal from bankruptcy. I believe I also threw in a few words on the fourteen freedoms. And out we went. We stayed under cover that night and the next. Early Monday morning I went to my union to explain the situation. Mr. de Lancey was there. Nothing happened. We'd lost the job and we didn't get our back pay. But it finally turned out bad for Tony too. The dancing school couldn't support both itself and the nite club and within a few months both closed down. A few years later Tony and I met in a lunch room, talked about old times like good friends, and reminisced about what might have been.

That quartet—Benny Moylan on tenor, Art on piano, Earl Murphy on banjo and guitar, Earl Wiley on drums—tried to make it as a band during the early thirties. Benny Moylan is a name most jazz fans won't know, because he died young and never recorded, but Art remembers him as a major talent.

I first met Benny Moylan on the train, going to a job in Racine, Wisconsin. He was around my height, five ten and a half, full of face in a lean sort of manner, nice smile. Benny tried to play tenor sax like Louis was playing trumpet at that time. He honked on it, got a tone like Pee Wee gets on clarinet, only considerably heavier. And he sang beautifully. Crosby reminds me of Benny, only Benny was hearing Louis all the time, and that's what would come out of him.

After that job in Racine we came back to Chi and Benny and I would hang out together. I had the use of a small organ—you know, the kind arrangers work out on, or the kind the Salvation Army uses—and I'd become pretty good at it. It's not an easy instrument to play on with a beat. Benny and I would stay home, or visit friends, and play. Once we went out on a strip of sand—you could stretch it a bit and call it a beach—and sat and played until we were scared off by the cops.

Too bad Benny never recorded. Benny and I made a few of the ten-cent variety of records while we were in Racine, but they warped on me, and though I tried my damnedest to dub them, it was impossible.

I believe Benny died at 27. He was in the hospital but wouldn't stay put; got out of bed saying, "Man, I'm not sick!" He was too strong to stay in bed, but it licked him; Benny went.

So you want to talk of tenor sax giants—so you go out and hear someone running up and down the scale, or play "Body and Soul," and you say "Oh, my God!" Well, we said that, years ago, when you had to be damn good before one of the boys said that about you. Ask Earl Murphy. You'll hear about a guy who could make you cry when he sang, and turn around and play you some low-down music on his sax (rubber bands and string attached) like you won't hear being played anywhere today.

After the taxi-dance job ended

Murphy got us a job at a spot about thirty miles outside of Chi. A lot of swanky people came there. Someone drove us out and we played for the boss. Besides playing as much music as any four pieces I've heard would produce, Benny sang. Wiley could do a dance, soft shoe, that would kill us. Murphy sang. I sang plenty too, and I'd written a song for a gangster that was very popular among that set. And when the boss found out I was the author—it was a dirty ditty—we were in.

After an audition the boss gave us a good salary, also $100 to get a car, so we could drive there and back, all we wanted to eat and drink. That's how it was when we started. But how we could drink! In a few days the bartenders couldn't take it. So new rules were laid down. A pint of gin when we got there; a pint of gin on the way home; in between a few drinks at the bar. Mind you, we were up there playing when we had to.

One night we were all packed up, in the car ready to drive off, when a few of the boss's cronies came in, wanting to hear my song. We got out the banjo and gave it to them right out in the yard, chorus after chorus. And he paid off, and we all split. But that ride home! Going there we wouldn't fight much about who drove the car we all owned, but coming back everyone was a race-track driver. We had a couple of close calls that I'd like to forget. And shortly I developed a bad set of nerves.

One day our place was held up. We were all on the stand playing when it happened. I found out later the hoodlums broke the doorman's head a bit, and ruined the chap's arm just to impress us. And then one of them slid across the dance floor up to the band with a gun pointed at us. "Get off and lay down, face forward." Needless to say, we did.

We'd just drawn fifty bucks to pay the union with, and Benny had it in his pocket. "Get up!" The band got up. "Empty your pockets!" Then Benny did something I'll always remember. "Man, we ain't got nothing—we're musicians—we're always broke—man, you know that. . . ." The hood sort of laughed and passed us by, but went down the line and took everyone else's bankroll. They also took everyone's car keys. Also they escorted a couple of girls out of the washroom. Those guys meant business.

It was a mess. All we could do was step up to the bar and drink—on the house. And I wrote another verse to my tune, about "Did you ever meet the hold-up man, Well into this cafe he ran, Pointed his gun, get off your————off the stand." After that the band was really set with the boss; we could have had anything.

But like all good things it came to an end. We started taking advantage a bit; we'd be late, and that would murder the boss. Once we had to lay Benny off for four days, rest him up a bit, figuring he'd need the job and behave when he got back. So we got Bud Freeman to take his place, just to help us out. But Bud wasn't happy in our sort of band. He heard notes, harmonies, we didn't play. And as for us, well, Bud was no Benny Moylan. Bud made pretty runs and knew his horn, but Benny was Louis on Gut Bucket. Benny honked on his tenor, he had a whiskey tone. He was in a groove that couldn't be mistaken. We sent for Benny to come back.

Three fellows in the band—all but me—had Irish in them, and you've heard of the fighting Irish. Well, when it got so bad that we took to talking of fighting between ourselves (this is all the way home, of course), and when Wiley pushed me through a plate glass door, just while emphasizing a point, I decided I needed a rest. Tut Soper took my place. But pretty soon I was back, too—and pretty soon we lost that job.

I worked on a couple more jobs with the four-piece band, and to show you how bad times were, one of us got a job at some club, some saloon, that paid us all of ten dollars a week apiece and all we could drink, and the second night the boss came over and says, "No more all you can drink."

One of the best jobs Art had during the depression was with the Floyd Towne band, at Harry's New York Bar, in 1935.

We had a four front line. Dick Donahue, the trumpet player. And Johnny Lane played clarinet. Bill Dohler was the alto man—awfully fine alto-saxophone player, never got the recognition I think he could have got had he desired to leave this town and go to New York. Floyd Towne was the tenor-saxophone player. Floyd Towne was a swimmer, an Olympic swimmer. And we had a bass player, Van Hook, who was very symphonically inclined, could play that way, and I think we had Jim Barnes on drums, and myself. And it was a very swinging band. We had air time, which was great. In those days being on the air was like being on TV today, and they used "Randolph Street Drag," that I wrote, as a theme when we'd go on the air. It was after that that I met Art Tatum and he told me he was in Cleveland, and he heard our band over the air, and the men in his band were telling him, "Listen to that black boy play piano," and he says, "I knew you wasn't black."

Harry's New York Bar stood where the Sun-Times Building is, in that area. It was the real nightclub scene. We played for dance, we played for acts. This is when I really started studying the piano, because that's when I ran up against a soprano singer, a coloratura singing arias, and I was lost. Nothin', I mean nothin' I ever encountered musically had prepared me for this experience. The piano had to carry the brunt of the music and I wasn't up to it. I really started studying, so I would know, so this wouldn't happen again to me, and I practiced four hours a night. Work eight hours, practice four on the job. Bill Dohler got on my case; I'll never be able to thank him enough. He not only showed me where I was lacking, he even found me a teacher, John Hawkins. He taught at the Fine Arts Building in the Loop.

He laid it out straight. "I've been teaching vocal for quite some time. I gave up teaching piano except in the one or two cases where the student is prepared to work at it seriously. I'll take you on, but believe me, you're going to have to really work, and work hard, just to catch up to where you should be at this stage of your career. It isn't going to be easy and you can quit any time. But if you stick with me I'll teach you."

I was determined. I'd received a deep shock that woke me up; you can bet I'd stick. But man oh man, I had no idea what I was letting myself in for. I had certain fingers that I hadn't really been using. Mr. Hawkins had special exercises for the likes of me. "I'm going to open up your hands so you'll get full use of them." You talk about fingers hollering at you, mine screamed. Sometimes the tears would come out of the corner of my eyes. I'd be down there in the sub-basement where that old upright piano stood. That's where I spent my intermissions; I mean every intermission. Slowly I began to get results. I would take a drink; I would get high. But I put my high to work for me. [Marijuana alters your sense of time, slows it down.] I would actually watch each finger and make it do what that exercise told it to do. All in all I stayed with my teacher some four years.

They had—we called them the three lovely boys. Elmer Schoebel— good pianist, he wrote a lot of tunes and arranged in those days—he played piano for two men singers that would make the rounds, who could handle just about any request thrown at them. If you wanted to cry in your beer they could turn that on, or turn right around and hit you with some jazz tune. They worked the intermission, and that would give me a chance to go downstairs. And when they'd start hitting on the floor with their canes I'd know they were about to get through and I'd better stop practicing and run upstairs. And then we'd be on again. I made use of that place; that place really worked for me. That was one of the best jobs at that time, but after that, outside of the Liberty Inn and the occasional one, things toughened up. You could really go without work. When Wingy left town he rode the rods— jumped the train to Florida or somewhere.

Art worked the Liberty Inn, at Clark and Erie Streets, many times. He had worked there with Wingy. He had worked there with the quartet, except with Gibby Eurton on guitar instead of Earl Murphy. And he was working there when he finally decided to leave Chicago for New York.

McGovern's Liberty Inn was the last of the bucket-of-blood joints. ["Three fights on week nights and five on the weekend," as Earl Wiley once put it. "If there was no fight nobody had any fun."] The Inn was unique because it kept running and being itself at a time when all other places had lost all identity—had just become upholstered sewers.

McGovern sure had a weakness for girlie pictures out front, the more the merrier. Old man McGovern was a sprightly white-haired man, and did he know the business! He didn't miss a bet. There was the time I was working there in the afternoons. Some guy came in for some innocent diversion, only he had about a grand on him. We had about six gals working there then, all sizes and all types. McGovern liked girls around. They worked on a percentage, so many drinks (phonies—"B"s, we called them) drunk a night, so much earned. Well, this unlucky guy comes in. I strike up a tune, some gay thing, and the big parade starts. First one gal sidles up to this fall guy; he doesn't give her a tumble. Then another, and still another. By this time he's downed several and is more amiable. Soon he latches on to one he likes, and soon she's warming him up, and he buys me one. And then she invites one of her "girlfriends" to join her, and pretty soon it's one big happy family, with our friend for the afternoon buying drinks for the house, about ten of us, and the drinks comin' so fast that nobody got a chance to drink except, of course, our indiscreet friend.

And somehow he passed out and had to be assisted upstairs. The hotel was right next door, also owned by McGovern. Didn't even have to go out of the bar: connecting door. And Mr. Grand was put to bed. And just before my shift was up he awoke, refreshed, but short of dough. Very short. He was very outspoken about it, but no one knew where it had strayed, except "Remember, you were buyin' everybody drinks? Remember?" And so he started drinking again, and fell off one of the stools. This time the dishwasher helped him up, but somehow his hand got caught in this man's pocket. But the man with the grand (minus) wasn't *that* drunk. He put up a squawk. So there was nothing for Old Man McGovern to do but fire the dishwasher. So he got his hat and coat on and with his head hanging low walked out—out past the front window to the side door that led back of the bar to the kitchen, where I later saw him back at work, washing dishes.

The McGoverns were a fighting Irish clan, and asked odds from no one. There was the time a tall husky Texan refused to pay the bill and started to fight about it. First Johnny and then Jim McGovern and then McCusak and a couple of others battled him from his table clear across the dance floor, during the middle of the show with the light on full blast. They battled and bustled him right through the door that led to the bar, and so into the men's room where the bill was collected. The porter mopped the blood on the dance floor and the show proceeded as scheduled.

And once a disgruntled customer threw a brick through the front window and ran. Johnny, who was about 5 feet 10 and weighed in the neighborhood of 140 pounds, chased him clear to Chicago Avenue, about four blocks, and about a hundred feet from a police station, caught up with him, and—well, that was that.

But the funny one was when some tough gal was gettin' too cantankerous for comfort, so she was handed a Mickey. And that's an art in itself, handing a party a Mickey without their getting wise to the fact. The bathrooms were then crowded with people, so that when Mr. Mickey started to work there was no—well, the result was that this female ran out into the nearest alley and was not heard of since.

Yes, the Liberty Inn was an education. But it was more than that. If you were one of them (and if you worked for them you were), then you knew where to go if you needed help, from brain to brawn.

The McGoverns liked jazz, and they hired jazz musicians, and the Liberty Inn became a jazz musicians' hangout, a place to hear good music, and a place to sit in.

Zurke came in there once and played a mess of piano. One time it was Marty Marsala, Wingy, Louis Prima, and Paul Mares all playing together—four trumpets. Dave Tough often came in. It was very painless moneywise. You could get a shot of gin for five cents if you was a musician. Imagine that. We really drew the musicians.

I remember the time that our drummer, Earl Wiley, who was a periodic drinker, decided that the period had arrived. Now Earl was one of the great drummers that I've played with. In the first place, he was a dancer, so he had the rhythm right into his feet. Earl was a riverboat drummer. He'd worked many circuses. He'd played tent shows and carnivals, up and down and to and fro. When those cootch dancers would get up and dance he would have to make the kind of beat that would stimulate them, and he'd really mastered that. And Earl was also great on woodblocks, and on playin' on the rims, things you don't hear much today.

When Earl started drinkin', everyone was his friend, and he bought drinks for everybody. And what the McGoverns did was follow him around, because they knew that sooner or later he would pick up his drums and take 'em to the nearest pawn shop and pawn 'em, and then they'd redeem the ticket, pick up the ticket. At the end of Earl's act, of course, usually they'd have to pump his stomach. I mean this man really would consume. And then after that he was all right—never touch a drop for the longest time, and be nice to get along with, too.

Well, this day we were gettin' ready to go on stage for the next set when someone remarked where was Earl. So the search was on. Soon someone found him in his room, in the hotel, and he was not so great. He was feeling no pain. So we had to get a sub, but fast. As luck would have it Davy Tough was in the room. He'd been listening and imbibing, but he looked OK. So here we go. But it didn't take long into that set to realize that Dave was in no shape to play. We managed to finish that bit, but the problem of a drummer for the rest of the night was still there. I don't know who it was that went after Wiley, but whoever it was told Earl, "Man, you better get back on stage; your sub is drunker than you are."

The Liberty Inn produced many incidents. Tut Soper—he's the

fellow who walked backwards into the Liberty Inn. He got on that kick of walking backwards. And there was the time the fellows in the band chipped in for a jug and sent Eddie Condon's brother Pat for it. And when we next heard from him he was in Australia.

The Liberty Inn was a good job because you got paid what for those days was a good eater, twenty-five, thirty, or thirty-five dollars a week, plus, if you wanted to hang in there and make the tips, that's when the money could be made, playing for singers. That meant playing from 10:00 to 1:00 in the back room.

The back room part of the Inn could seat somewhere in the vicinity of one hundred people. Music would start at 10:00. The band would play a short dance. Then the pianist in the band rolled a small piano onto the middle of the dance floor and a couple of entertainers would make the rounds of the tables and come back with the folding money, if they were lucky, of which you'd get your share—half, if you kept your eyes on them. As I was developing the habit of playing with my eyes shut so as to concentrate more on my music, quite often I lost out in the other department, and got ribbed by the help about being a sucker. Well, after playing for the singers you dragged the piano back and played another dance. This went on till the show started. Then, of course, you played the show. The show was a killer—one singer, one comedian (the MC) and four strip girls. The place did good business, everything moved along at a given pace, but all in all it was a grind for the man at the piano.

So that was a good job. But outside of that things weren't that easy. And meanwhile big bands were coming in, three saxophones and stuff, and the arranger was becoming known. Radio was beginning to feature more and more of the larger groups, and the small band wasn't being heard. The accordion was beginning to replace the piano. And the small groups that would entertain—you were beginning to hear the agent say, "What else do you do? Do you tell jokes? Do you wear funny hats? Do you dance? What do you *do* besides play music?"

This was what started that exodus, long before I left. Before I left for New York Condon had left. Red McKenzie, who hung around Chicago for a while, he'd left. Mezz had left; Bud Freeman had left; Gene Krupa had left; even George Wettling. They'd all left to try the New York scene. And we were still struggling with Chicago, trying to make it, hanging in there, and it was getting harder. It was scuffling more, for a job, for a buck. And New York was being written up in *down beat*, you know, like there was gold on those streets.

7

Paying the New York Dues

One reason the hot men could survive through the worst years of the depression was that

most of us had no family. It didn't take much for us to get by, and that's all anyone was doing, gettin' by. Like ten bucks a week you had you a room with privileges. Two bucks got you Pete's best tea (marijuana, arrangements) in a Prince Albert can. The music was so important to us, so other things fell into place. If you ate, you ate. If you didn't, well, you made it. But somehow it seemed like we did eat and we did have a car and we did get around and we listened to what we wanted to listen to.

But Art had married early in 1938. When he and Thelma arrived in New York they weren't friendless. There were the Chicago hot men who had left before them, and there was an old friend Art had roomed with in his bachelor days, Bill Kennedy,

one of the fellows I met through Wingy Manone, when we lived on Lawrence Avenue, on the North Side of Chicago. There was a little colony of New Orleans fellows that lived near us, and mostly they were bellhops or race-track touts. And one of these New Orleans people that I liked real well and got acquainted with was Bill Kennedy, and he was a professional fighter, in fact he fought all the way to the top of his profession. He was a lightweight. Well, when I knew Bill he was tryin' to make a comeback, kind of half-heartedly. And he enjoyed the music.

We were living in an apartment on the North Side, you know, community bathroom, and Bill went into the bathroom and whoever lived next door to us hadn't kept it very clean. So he hung up a sign — he was very direct — he says, "Hey you pigs, just because you are doesn't mean you have to live like them"—hoping they'd get the message. Well, they got the message, all right, and how I found it out was we were sittin' in the room and somebody says, "Gee, we're out of cigarettes." And I says, "Well, I'm tired of sittin'; I'll go to the corner and get you some." And just as I turned the corner somebody stuck a hand out, with a fist attached, and the next thing you know I was picking myself up, six feet away, out of the curb. It was one of these cats, and there was about half a dozen of them. And they thought it was very funny; they all stood there and laughed.

I says, "I don't think it's so funny; I'm goin' back and get some help." I came back with about four of the New Orleans guys, and these guys disappeared; they wanted no part of us. Well, you know how New Orleans cats are; they think about these things, and one of their people had been attacked. They weren't gonna let that go. About a half hour later they walked out. This time they caught this guy. Well, it wasn't pretty. In fact the cops came and wanted to know who had the knife. There was no knife.

This was Bill Kennedy, and when he went to New York City he talked to me right along that this was the place I should be. He said, "You can move in with me till you get started." Well, later I took him at his word. I just packed all my belongings, my wife, and my two dogs, and we descended on Bill in his apartment. And without a word he put us up.

New York was a complete revelation from what Chicago was. One of the first places I visited was the Hickory House, on 52nd Street, where Joe Marsala had the band. That was a prize job and Joe had a good group. Buddy Rich was his drummer and Marty Marsala blew trumpet. And Eddie Condon was playin' guitar. That's the first time I saw musicians playin' for kicks with an audience and gettin' paid. You got to remember that in Chicago musicians played for acts or dancing. There was a social order in night clubs and musicians were pretty close to the bottom of the scale. Usually the show girls, star acts, MC were number one. Bartenders and waiters ranked next. Of course the bandleader rated, but not the sidemen. We came a notch above the washroom attendants. Fact. You could work a joint and practically go unnoticed. The acts would know you by your instrument: "Give the piano player this music," never, "Hand this to Art."

There were occasional exceptions. When the Floyd Towne band broad-

cast from Harry's New York Bar, fan mail came in from radio listeners, and Harry moved the band off the wall and onto the floor and gave them a feature number in the show. "That's when we started being noticed," says Art. "We'd get individual hellos when we came to work." Or there would be an occasional public jam session at a musicians' hangout, like My Cellar.

But that was rare. No one paid especially to hear music played, except on the South Side of Chicago, if it was a black neighborhood and a black band. Those people were very informed about what they were coming for—to listen. They didn't need anything else.

But white audiences—it was a tremendous surprise to see a room full of people sitting there listening to a group of musicians perform. So walking in there I was stunned. And Joe says, "Come on, sit in." I think that's the first time I got stage fright. But I sat in, and there was a fellow by the name of Herman Rosenberg there, and he caught the set I played and I guess he was very impressed because he put in *down beat* that a new Chicago pianist had hit town, and that Jess Stacy and Joe Sullivan better watch out. It was really to laugh, because I had two more years of just struggling to find work, just to be able to play, before anybody had to worry about me.

I was down at the union, Local 802, the first weekday after we arrived in New York City. The American Federation of Musicians has a rule that says a member must present a traveling card to whatever local he descends on, if he wants to work in that jurisdiction. I did what I was told. My card was accepted and I got my instructions. For the first three months I could not work any place where a steady band was employed. Nor was I allowed to leave the jurisdiction. I could take any job I could find provided it was a one-time engagement, like a wedding or a dance. If I was caught doing anything but what I was instructed to do I would have to leave the territory and not come back to try again for another year. In that way this local tried to protect itself against out-of-town musicians coming in and taking the work away from the local talent.

Well, that's a tough diet. You run all over hell and creation to play a one-nighter. You turn down an offer to join Bunny Berigan because his gigs are taking him out of town, and you want to stay and sweat your card out. Not that you don't have connections, guys that want to help you, players you knew back in Chicago, like Joe Marsala.

"Pops," he'd say, "I'll give you a night's work. Don't worry about the union." The next evening I got dressed in my tux, ready to go to work. Then came the knock on the door. I opened it and some man I never saw before came in and introduced himself. He was a union agent (I was to discover they had some thirty of them) and he was "just checking. And where are you going in a tuxedo? Where you working?" I told him I had a wedding job. He couldn't disprove it, but he could follow me when I left the house, and everywhere I looked I saw a pair of eyes staring at me. I ducked every which way before I grabbed a subway and made it to 52nd Street, and I was a wreck when I arrived at the Hickory House. No way would I go to work. I hope Joe understood.

Art and Thelma eventually found an apartment of their own, and Art picked up occasional jobs, but even after the probationary period had passed, and Art was working more than one-nighters,

we were really scuffling, digging underneath the bottom. Thelma had borne our first child, Janet, in New York, and she decided, I've got a baby, and it's more important that she has milk than that I stick it out here with you, and she went back to Chicago for a while, so for the next three months I moved in with Dick Donahue, the trumpet player from the Floyd Towne band, and we tried to make it.

He had many saving graces. One of them was that he liked to cook, and his main dish was a soup-stew: a soup bone with meat attached, a dime for this or a quarter for that. Never forget the twenty-five-cent pint of wine. We fed a lot of Chicago musicians; five or six would drop by any time and taste our stew.

Donahue met a drummer, Joe Grauso, and Joe came up with a three-piece job in the lower Village: Dick on trumpet, myself on piano, and Joe on drums. Now business wasn't too good there; we were making four bucks a night apiece, and our union decided to picket because the place was unfair. Well, they started picketing the place, and we shouldn't be there, but we needed the bread. So as the pickets would walk in different directions we would run out for our little bottle of wine. Then we'd wait for them to come together, and when they'd walk apart we'd run in again. But business was bad, bad enough so the pickets stopped picketing; there was no need for them.

One night when I came to work Dick wasn't there. The boss says, "I sent him home, and I sent the drummer home too. There's just you on piano." Well, it was better for one of us to work than none. So I played single. A party came in of about ten people. I watched them sittin' around, waiting for service. Finally I walked over to the boss and asked him where's the waiter. He informed me, "You're the waiter." Well, four bucks. I walked over to that table and proceeded to take their orders. I got that part straight, but when I returned and tried to sort out what drink belonged to whom, that was it. One of the customers politely asked me, "What else do you do?" Then he suggested, "Why don't you go play the piano; we'll serve ourselves." And that was the last of that job.

During that time Frankie Laine and I got together. He was trying to make it as a singer; he sang two nights a week at the Hickory House. Joe really didn't need him but he felt sorry for the cat because he wanted to sing that bad. We were a team; we put in about two years starvin' together. He could swing, and he was ambitious. We would haunt the agencies just to audition. You talk about knockin' at doors, Frankie would bust them open. "Let me go in and talk; I can get by that gal at the desk." And he would. Any number of nite spots in New Jersey gave us employment. We worked it up from ten dollars a date between us to fifty apiece a week. Somewhere along the line I taught him to sing "My Desire," which eventually was the song that took him to a measure of stardom. We had a hard time gettin' along because we both had supreme egos. I was never happy with the billing; I thought it should be "Hodes and Laine." Eventually it was the bickering that broke us up. Maybe fifty dollars apiece was too rich for our blood. I have no bad feelings to look back on as far as he was concerned. Frankie was kind—always asked how my family was makin' it. He shared.

New York is a cold town, you know, mostly because everybody's so busy tryin' to get somewhere they're aiming at, and they just don't have time. And you pay your dues in New York, you know. Because although the subway fare may be a nickel, though the nickel hot dog is around, still you got to put in your time until you get known. And although you're bound to cry great big tears about how tough this town is, somehow you make it, and you find people, and you find places.

I had a problem of finding a piano to play on; it was very important. I knew sometime or other I would get a chance, or at least I thought I would, but I'd have to be able to play when that time came, and you know there was no piano in our apartment. One day LeRoy Smith, the clarinet player, called me up, and I met him at a joint he told me of, the Ross Tavern, 51st and Sixth Avenue. He introduced me to Jimmy Ross, who was a friend of George Zack, the pianist.

Jimmy Ross was an Irishman who had graduated from Notre Dame, and naturally when you graduate from Notre Dame and you're an Irishman you open up a tavern. And he was a frustrated musician; he'd played the violin. But he really loved the players, and he says, "Well come on, man, I got a piano in my basement. You just come down and play it." I never will forget that basement, because they had several cats running around, and they had those great big water buffaloes, you know what I mean, those great big black roaches running down there. So the cats would chase the roaches, and I would try to warm up on that piano and forget that whole scene. That was really a dreadful place in many ways, but you could play and play, get lost in your music. No interruptions; no requests.

Jimmy Ross was somethin' else. That kind of guy you don't stumble on every day. There was a great big hole kicked in one of the walls down in that basement. How I found out was the piano got moved to cover the hole. I was curious, and the story I was told went like this. Sometimes at the end of the evening Jimmy would be so fractured that he'd decide to sleep it off downstairs. Flopped on a table and passed out. During the morning he awoke, and it was pitch dark. Started feeling his way along the walls. "Let me out of here. Damn it, let me out." Of course there was no one to hear him. That's when he started kicking at the wall. And I remember the time he decided to go on the wagon and he was cuttin' lemons and near cut his little finger off. Drinking he could handle it; sober he was all thumbs.

It was in the late thirties that the first knowledgeable white audience for jazz was forming in the United States. Two editions of Delaunay's Hot Discography *were published; Stephen Smith founded the Hot Record Society;* Jazzmen *was published; the first of the small jazz record companies—Blue Note, Commodore, and Solo Art—began operations; the first of the jazz little magazines,* Jazz Information, *was being published. Several of the leaders of this movement began to hang out in Ross's basement.*

I came and I played. The thing lasted the best part of a winter. When it got around to Dan Qualey of Solo Art records and then to the *Jazz Information* gang, Gene Williams, Ralph Gleason, and Herman Rosenberg, the exact date I don't know. But that gang came to listen, and they brought life into that cellar.

It started to attract musicians. I heard Meade "Lux" Lewis come down and play some piano, George Zack, and a vocalist by the name of Stella Brooks. Stella was just a little bit of a gal, but she had that brain, that ego-power that could turn people on. One of her followers was Billie Holiday. Every time I'd be around Stella, Billie Holiday would come over, almost like she was coming to get her directional signals. Stella just turned her on; she had a lot of quips and she was fast. She was sort of a female Eddie Condon.

With Stella it never turned into work; we never got close to a gig. But we made lots of music together. The basement of Ross Tavern suited her just fine. So she'd come down there and sing, and I played for her. The drinks would flow; whoever had the money would pay. On occasion Ross would send down a pitcher of beer. Everything got quiet while the music went on—talk about your playing for keeps. Like I say, Jimmy Ross gave me a place to play, and it got pretty well known. So if you have a need and you really want to there's a way that doors open.

So it was fitting that when Qualey asked me to record for his Solo Art label we met at Ross's and warmed up. At that time recording for Solo Art was big time for me. I'd only cut one record before that, and that was in Wingy Manone's band; now I was to get a shot at a piano solo recording. And dig this—Danny had never recorded a white pianist before. Nor after, not to my knowledge, although he tried real hard with George Zack. Cripple Clarence Lofton, Meade Lux, Albert Ammons, Pete Johnson. I was in exclusive company.

No LPs then; you cut one record and it better be good. We made five tracks, out of which Dan selected two: "South Side Shuffle" and "Ross Tavern Boogie." Later Dan substituted a second track for "South Side Shuffle," still calling it by the same title. That was one real breakthrough for me in the jazz world. In the December issue of *Columbia '39*, a university paper, Ralph Gleason reported that "Qualey is about to issue solos by an extraordinary white pianist, Art Hodes. A real oldtimer [I was in my thirties], Hodes is the only white man to play real boogie-woogie. In the blues tradition his sincerity and purity of style tops any white pianist of today."

down beat (June 1940) picked it in its "Best Solos on the Wax." What I had put down was the music I had been playing nightly at

Ross's Tavern, blues with a boogie beat. It came out for real because I was talkin' from inside, tellin' it how it was with me. And I came to that recording date with the right climate. I could spill you some blues. I was feelin' it all the way.

1. Art Hodes at the piano, New York, in the forties.

2. Art and his mother, Dorothy, late 1926 or early 1927. Art was about to leave Chicago for the first time, to tour with Dick Voynow's Wolverine Orchestra.

3. The Floyd Towne band at Harry's New York Bar, Chicago, 1935. Standing, left to right: Floyd Towne, tenor; Jim Barnes, drums; Norman Van Hook, bass; Johnny Lane, clarinet; Art Hodes, piano. Seated: Dick Donohue, trumpet; Bill Dohler, alto. "Towne" was originally "Town"; numerology was responsible for the change, as it was with Wingy "Manone" (from "Mannone") and "Georg Brunis" (from "George Brunies").

4. Mezz Mezzrow and Art at Ryan's. They are clearly into it; the anonymous member of the audience seems out of it.

5. The Art Hodes Trio at Jimmy Ryan's, on 52nd Street, in the forties: Danny Alvin, drums; Mezz Mezzrow, clarinet; Art Hodes, piano; and Jimmy Ryan, the former Broadway bit player who managed the club. Photograph by Chilton-Butler, Ridgewood, N.J.

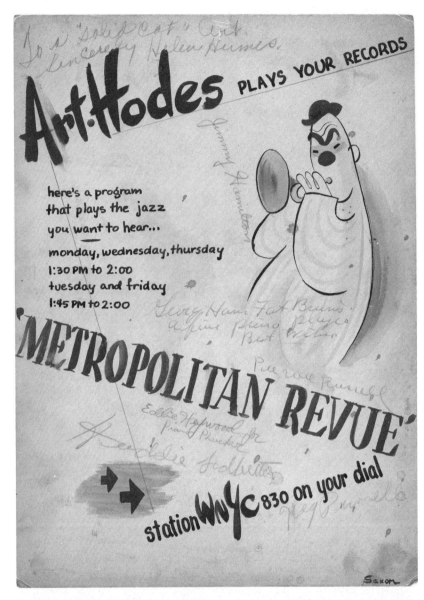

6. A poster for Art's WNYC radio show in the forties, by Saxon. The autographs, from top to bottom, are by Helen Humes, Jimmy Hamilton, "George Ham Fat Brunis," Pee Wee Russell, Eddie Heywood, Jr., Huddie Ledbetter ("Leadbelly"), and Meg Purnell.

7. Art in the office of the *Jazz Record* magazine, in the mid-forties. Photograph by Ed Rice.

8. Issue No. 40 of the *Jazz Record*, January 1946. The photograph of Sidney Bechet is by Francis Wolff of Blue Note records.

9. Darnell Howard, clarinet; Frankie Newton, trumpet; and Art Hodes, piano, at a jam session in the Village.

BLUE NOTE PRESENTS
AT TOWN HALL, 123 West 43rd Street
SATURDAY, DECEMBER 15, 5:30 P.M.

JAMMING IN JAZZ
WITH AMERICA'S GREAT JAZZ MEN

ART HODES
SIDNEY BECHET
SIDNEY DE PARIS
SANDY WILLIAMS
ALBERT NICHOLAS
DANNY ALVIN
WELLMAN BRAUD

SINGING THE BLUES:
"PIGMEAT" MARKHAM
COW COW DAVENPORT

SIDNEY CATLETT
FRANKIE NEWTON
SAMMY BENSKIN
JIMMY SHIRLEY
BILLY TAYLOR

NARRATION BY FRED ROBBINS

Tickets on sale at box office

B L U E
NOTE

10. A flyer for a concert at Town Hall, in the forties.

11. A flyer for "Jazz on the River," a series of gigs organized by Art and Rudi Blesh.

12. Part of the "Jazz on the River" band, with friends. Standing, left to right: Danny Barker, guitar and banjo; Albert Nicholas, clarinet; Wild Bill Davison, cornet; writer and promoter Rudi Blesh; writer Bob Aurthur. Seated, left to right: Art Hodes, piano; Baby Dodds, drums; designer Jimmy Ernst. Blesh and Aurthur both wrote for the *Jazz Record*; Ernst, son of the painter Max Ernst, designed some of its covers.

13. Seated, left to right, at a New York club in the forties: unknown; Cow Cow Davenport, piano; Art Hodes, piano; Pops Foster, bass; Baby Dodds, drums.

14. The Hodes family at home in West Hempstead, Long Island, in the late forties. From left to right: Art; his father, William; Janet; Karen; Thelma; Bob. Photograph by K. Christian Lenskold, Floral Park, N.Y.

15. Jimmy Durante visits with Art and Jimmy Granato, the clarinetist in Art's band, Chicago, 1951. Durante began his career as a pianist with the Original New Orleans Jazz Band, which recorded for Okeh in 1918 and for Gennett in 1919. Aside from Durante the musicians were in fact from New Orleans, and because the clarinetist, Achille Baquet, was a Creole passing for white, it may have been the first mixed jazz band to record. Granato played New York's Palace Theatre with Durante in 1929; Durante is pointing to a crack made in the bell of Granato's clarinet by a flying telephone flung across the stage by Durante in one of the more exuberant moments of that engagement. *Chicago Daily News* photograph, courtesy of the *Chicago Sun-Times*.

16. The rhythm section of Art's band at Rupneck's in the fifties: Buddy Smith, drums; Earl Murphy, bass; Art Hodes, piano. It was Earl Murphy who introduced Art to jazz through his record collection, at Delavan Lake, in the summer of 1927. Buddy Smith's associations spanned much of jazz history. His uncle, Andrew Hilaire, played drums on Jelly Roll Morton's first Victor recordings; Buddy himself played with Charlie Parker.

17. The band at the Turf Club, Indianapolis, 1957: Art Hodes, piano; Buddy Smith, drums; Jimmy Granato, clarinet; Muggsy Dawson, cornet; Bill Johnson, trombone. Photograph by William L. Clouse, Associated Photographers.

18. Recording for educational television in the studio of WTTW, Chicago, 1969-71: Art Hodes, piano; Barney Bigard, clarinet; Rail Wilson, bass; Bob Cousins, drums.

19. Another WTTW program: Art Hodes, piano; Pee Wee Russell, clarinet; Jimmy McPartland, cornet.

20. Art at WTTW.

21. Art Hodes, piano; Doc Evans, trumpet; Bob Cousins, drums; at WTTW.

22. Program cover for the quartet that toured for Columbia Artists in the seventies.

23. Setting up for a European concert: Nice Jazz Festival, 1975. Photograph by Hans Harzhelm, Dusseldorf.

24, 25, and 26.
At an outdoor concert in Chicago's Loop, in the seventies, Art responds to the music (24 and 25) and so does his audience (26). Photographs by Chadwick Hansen.

27 and 28. Art and Jan Hodes at the piano, Toronto, September 1987. Photographs copyright by Paul J. Hoeffler, Toronto.

29. An ad from the two-year gig at the Mayfair-Regent Hotel, Chicago, early eighties.

8

Spreading the Good Word

Art would record ten more sides during 1940: two solos, four trio sides, and four with a band. The solos, two of his best recordings, were made because George Zack's attention wandered when Dan Qualey tried to record him for Solo Art.

Dan really wanted to get George on his label. He had the studio booked. And George says, "I tell you what, Dan, let's stop at a pub and have a few drinks. I just want to get into the spirit of the thing. So Dan says, "Fine. OK." So they had a few drinks, and Dan says to George, "Are you ready now?" And George says, "Yeah, anything is all right." So Dan says, "Well, I'll call up the studio and say we're on our way." In the ten minutes it took him to go and call, George kept drinking, and when Dan came back he was out of the mood. "Not now," he says. "Later." Well, you can't do that with studio time. When you got it booked you make use of it or you find yourself payin' for it. So I was the substitute choice. And I made a tune called "Selection from the Gutter," which is one of my best blues.

The other side was "Organ Grinder Blues." The record never appeared on Solo Art; Dan Qualey ran out of money shortly after it was recorded. Eventually it was issued on Bob Thiele's Signature label, and later reissued on Milt Gabler's Commodore. It had been recorded in March 1940 (or maybe January; the exact date is uncertain). The trio sides were made in May, the band sides in August. The trios were recorded because

Bob Thiele was a Rod Cless fan. As I understand it he was taking clarinet lessons from Cless. One day Rod approached me with the idea of a recording date from Thiele. It was to be a trio. I got Jimmy Butts on bass and we cut a date. This was received so well that several months later we were back in the studio, this time with a larger group. We'd added Marty Marsala on trumpet and Jack Goss on guitar. Earl Murphy took over the bass. We had George Wettling slated to play drums, but at the last minute he couldn't make it and sent a sub. I told the drummer no, never having played with him, I couldn't pick that time to run experiments. So we recorded without drums. Had to work a little harder. When the record was released and I got a chance to hear it I was standing in Steve Smith's H.R.S. record shop. A well-known jazz writer was attracted by the music and came over. He said, "You guys were really swinging. Who's that on drums?"

In the spring of 1940 Art played in a trio at Jimmy Ryan's, with Mezz Mezzrow on clarinet, and in the fall he led his first New York jazz band, in a restaurant near Columbia University.

There was a booking agent by the name of Freddie Williamson. I don't know how he got my name, but he called me one day and offered me this job at a Childs' Restaurant at 103rd and Broadway. They're pretty much all over New York. They're not expensive places to eat, but they're nice.

The manager was a young man. He greeted me, sat me down with a cup of coffee, and told me what he wanted. "Art, Freddie recommends you highly. To tell you the truth, after 9 P.M. we're not doing much business. Fred says you have a following, and although we've never played jazz in this place we're willing to give it a try. Monday through Saturday you go from seven to nine. Back at ten to one. Now then, look around you. See that nice old lady sitting there? She's been coming here for years. See that white scale on the counter? We measure out her food in calories. Now we don't want to run her out with your music. So from seven to nine you play soft. Romantic. Waltzes. A little Spanish. You can operate the lights to change the mood. But when you come back at ten I don't care what you play. I don't care if you shit on the floor, just as long as you do business."

Freddie had suggested I use George Brunis, not that I needed prodding. I wanted Rod Cless. Piano, trombone, clarinet. We got Joe Grauso on drums and Duke DuVal on trumpet. We called the group the Columbia Quintet. My two jazz greats split the leader's money equally with me; that made it $42.50 apiece and $35 for each of the sidemen. We came to work at seven and played waltzes or tangos and rhumbas, Brunis operating the lights and Cless with the maracas or bongo sticks.

Rod and George would switch, so we'd have all kinds of lighting effects and all kinds of rhythmic effects, while the piano played the melody. It was really a strange scene. But stranger still, we enjoyed it. Probably rested our stomachs. And I'll tell you somethin' else. In the time we were there we never ran that woman out, that woman with the white scales.

We had a locker downstairs we could repair to and drink some supper. Ten o'clock, a new deal. You wouldn't recognize that band. We'd come upstairs and open up with "Muskrat Ramble." The walls would shake. We drew a lot of students from Columbia University, which was practically around the corner, plus the jazz writers, like Gene Williams, Ralph Gleason, Herman Rosenberg. George Avakian would hang his hat there. Dan Qualey of Solo Art. They beat the drums and led an audience to Childs. Applause, encores, attendance, we had it. From ten till quittin' time the place was populated. We had a success.

After we were there ten weeks we decided we needed new material. That called for a rehearsal, and as we got set to rehearse the manager called me over and gave me my two-week notice. You know its dangerous to call rehearsals. Another way to lose a gig is to take band pictures, or record the band. So there went that job. It wasn't our fault. The students had discovered they could come in the front door, have something to eat, and disappear out the side door, so though we packed the place the register didn't show it. The place was losing money and wasn't aware of why. I wonder if they ever got wise?

down beat ran a headline: "Hodes Would Rather Eat Than Starve, So He Junks His Band." It was a nice headline, but actually I had very little to do with junking the band. I mean, we lost the Childs' 103rd Street gig. That was my first band in New York, and that was the last jazz band I ever had where it had to be all one color. Quickly I discovered New York's one union meant you could have a mixed band if you were willing to stand up for your beliefs and desires. [Chicago, like most American cities, had two musicians' unions, one for whites and one for blacks, until after the Second World War.]

Back in Chicago, there were always bands "rehearsing." In New York City I learned, first get the job, or at least the angle. The men? You'll find 'em. There were always more jazz musicians than places for them to play. The book? You speak the same language, got it memorized, stamped into you. How many times have I heard people say, "You guys sound good; how long you been together?" Huh? A couple of phone calls had gathered the brood.

At the moment, however, Art was out of a job, so

I tried a mickey foursome for a short time at a small club called the Pepper Pot, in the Village. My agent, Fred Williamson, said, "This is a chance for you to work. It's not the kind of job you just had, but you'll be able to make a living." It was a four-piece combo: clarinet, piano, guitar and bass, the kind of band that could do the job, play any tune that the people wanted to hear. We played a lot of pop tunes of that day, or standard tunes, for dancing mostly. It was the kind of band that was always there on time. Always dressed neatly. Fit into the woodwork and gave no one any problems. Playing music they never perspired. So it was almost like a rest cure except that it was also very boring. I didn't get happy there.

I discovered that they had an upper floor to this Pepper Pot, so during intermission I'd go up to that upper floor, and I'd have a beat-up piano, and I'd sit and play the piano for my kicks. Freddie Williamson, the ten percenter, the agent, joined me, and we proceeded to drink. The place even had a dumbwaiter; we could order our drinks and have them run up by the dumbwaiter. And I'd sit there and play till it was time for me to go to work. Well, that job didn't last long. I got sick of playing with fellows that did everything right except play.

So here I was in between. When you played with the hot men, the jazz players, you were liable to lose jobs. But when you played with people who were straight, as far as attendance, and the things that customers look for in musicians, you lose hope.

The next thing to do is to go to work alone. I found a little place in the Village where I could work alone, and the boss really dug my playing. And he had an idea: "Maybe I could get two pianists." I says, "Well, why don't you get George Zack. He's in New York. He's a very fine piano player." He says, "I want to tell you a story about George, because I had the idea to get George, too. In fact, some time ago I contacted George, and I got him a room in the hotel, and I said, 'George, I'm goin' to get you dressed up, and I'm goin' to give you this job, and you gonna enjoy it because you gonna be able to play just what you want to play. So George, I'm gonna get your measurements, get you dressed, and meanwhile, if you want anything just pick up the phone.' There went the job, 'cause when I left, George picked up the phone, and called for room service, and proceeded to get drunk. That lost his attention." Needless to say, George and I never got together on the double piano job.

Art would occasionally play solo again, but more often he led his own band. He led many bands in many New York clubs throughout the forties, and he developed a talent for jazz leadership in another way: he began what would become a long career of writing and speaking to the public about jazz. He had been impressed by the little community of record collectors and jazz critics he had met at Ross's Tavern.

For the first time in my life in jazz, I found people who weren't players taking a hand in helping the music exist, people who put much effort in furthering it, people that loved the jazz, weren't looking to make a buck off it, just loved it for itself.

They had been even more impressed by him, not only by his music, but also by his being that rare phenomenon, an articulate musician, one who spoke as he played, directly and with authority. So they thought of him when the only jazz program on WNYC, New York City's public radio station, was in danger of going out of existence.

Ralph Berton, a brother of that fine drummer, Vic, had a jazz program, a show called "The Metropolitan Review," on WNYC. He'd been doin' it for two years, and the word was he was retiring. Gene Williams and Ralph Gleason, the *Jazz Information* boys, decided that I should be the one to carry on. One day they asked me would I be interested. They says, "If someone doesn't take it over it's gonna go the way of all flesh. It'll disappear from the scene, and we need it, that outlet for jazz." I says, "I never did anything like this." They says, "Well, try it, we'll help you." So they took me down to New York City's own station, and I auditioned, and I got the show. You were on six days a week, for half an hour, at 1:30. No show on Sunday, but on Saturday you had an hour show.

In a half-hour show I had to have eight records and copy, notes written down. Now when I first took that show I had my little wind-up victrola, like all the other musicians, and about twenty-five records that I always carried around, maybe a few more. Gene and Ralph supplied me with records and wrote me a script, daily. All I had to do was talk. And I could play the piano, too. We used Louis Armstrong's intro to "West End Blues" as my theme, and usually I played myself off the air. Saturday afternoons I had guests. And in no time I had a lot of listeners, thousands of younger people, plus the players who got up in the middle of the night (1:30 in the afternoon) to give a listen. I remember Pee Wee Russell telling me, "I catch your show all the time. Keeps me from having to play my records."

I featured things the other stations didn't play: King Oliver, the Dodds brothers, Jimmie Noone, Earl Hines, Jelly Roll Morton; such pianists as Jimmy Yancey, Pine Top Smith, Fats Waller, James P. Johnson. I was playing the records I wanted to hear; I enjoyed doing the show. And in no time, like two or three months, I began to feel my oats, and I felt like I ought to be able to say more than I'm sayin', and I'd start to stray from the script. That's why I lost Gene and Ralph, and I don't blame 'em, lookin' back. Of course it made my way a little harder to go. That's what made a record collector out of me, because now I needed to have my hands on more records. In no time at all I was the owner of several hundred 78s.

Other people came around and started helpin' me, though. Now this job didn't pay nothin'; WNYC is a not-for-profit station. I paid my own subway fares to get there, bought or brought my own lunch. And the recordings were either my own or had been loaned to me by friends. All the station offered me was a turntable with needle attached, plus an announcer (for a while he was Jack Lescoulie). This being a work of love the New York musicians' union allowed me to use musicians, let the fellows come on and play, so I had all kinds of great musicians helpin' me out. Eddie Condon and his whole gang: Pee Wee, Brad Gowans, Max Kaminsky, Wettling, Joe Sullivan. Miff Mole, Tony Parenti, Mezzrow. I'd have Red Allen, who'd bring Higgy and Stovall. James P. Johnson appeared. Leadbelly. I can't remember all the names.

I could never have handled that show alone; the musicians were the greatest. Ditto the collectors, guys like Herb Abramson, who a bit later on was to help found Atlantic Records. "Would ya like me to bring Cow Cow Davenport up?"

Abramson asked on one occasion. Of course Art was delighted to have the pioneering boogie-woogie pianist on his show. Davenport was down on his luck; after a long career in black music and black vaudeville, he was the washroom attendant at the Onyx Club, on 52nd Street. One of the genuinely important achievements of the group of collectors and jazz critics of which Art had become a part was to rediscover some of the older black jazz and blues musicians and to provide an audience for them.

Eventually "The Metropolitan Review" went off the air.

We had a tremendous audience. A lot of kids listened to us. Unfortunately we also had another listener, the Little Flower, the late Mayor LaGuardia. He who liked to chase the fires. Most of the time I came on long after he'd been on the air, but one time he had to go on after me, so my program was being beamed while he was waiting to go on, and he heard. He heard me sayin', "This is a Decca record, and I'd give the number. He let out a scream, "Get that bum off the air! He's commercial!"

He didn't know that I didn't get the record from Decca. I had to buy the record. And how could I answer the letters that I'd get askin' me what was that record that you played? I didn't have a secretary. It made my job simpler if I could anticipate such questions over the air. The mayor never saw it that way, nor could I get the message across to him. I was warned then not to mention labels. For a while I cooled it, but eventually I fell back into the old style. And eventually he was on the air again after me, and there went the gig. They got the bum off the air. There was a lot of heat generated, and many letters poured into WNYC. All to no avail. I could resign or get fired. I slid off gracefully. But while I was there I accomplished a lot. If you're not sure about the need for jazz programs on radio, tune in. It's barren. If it were food, I wouldn't eat it; if it were a book, I wouldn't read it. Why do we settle for such trash where our ears are concerned?

The letters and phone calls from his audience had given Art his first full view both of the public's ignorance of jazz and of the willingness of part of it to learn, so when "Dale Curran—a printer by trade, an editor by inclination, a jazz lover, a man who had written two novels about jazz, Dupree Blues *and* Piano in the Band—*came up with the idea that we should put out a magazine together," Art was receptive. The two of them published and edited* The Jazz Record *from February 1943 to November 1947, a total of sixty issues, with Curran dropping out during the last year and Art carrying on with the aid of Harold Hersey.*

Initially the aims were modest: it was primarily a newsletter, telling the public where the music could be heard, reviewing new jazz records, and acting as a medium of exchange for record collectors. Very early, however, it began to bridge the gap between the musicians and the public in another fundamental way—telling the musicians' stories. In part this was done through the conventional technique of having a critic or aficionado do a biographical article. More importantly, it was done in two ways no other magazine had ever tried. First, Art wrote his own autobiographical articles, full of the people, the places, and the music that had made up his life. Second, he brought other musicians to the office, sat them down with a drink, and persuaded them to tell their own stories, while Curran, who was a speed typist, took down what they said. The result was an important body of oral history, created before that technique was in general use among professional historians. It has been a major source for subsequent jazz history, and in 1977 the University of California Press published an anthology from it, Selections from the Gutter, *edited by Art and myself.*

Art once said there were "beautiful stories" in the Jazz Record, *and so there were: the only autobiographical accounts of Cow Cow Davenport; reminiscences of Bessie Smith by Art, by Zutty Singleton, and by Carl Van Vechten, with Van Vechten's great photograph of Bessie on the cover; George Wettling's memories of Baby Dodds at Kelly's Stable; Omer Simeon's account of recording with Jelly Roll Morton. And there is Jim Robinson's account of himself: "I like to see people happy. If everyone is in a frisky spirit, the spirit gets to me and I can make my trombone sing. . . . It gives me a warm heart and that gets into my music. . . . I try to give my feelings to the other fellow. That's always in my mind. . . . Just keep living and loving your music and keep no evil in your heart."*

9

The Jazz Wars

The Jazz Record *centered on the musicians rather than on abstract criticism. The cover of the first issue carried a photograph of Kaiser Marshall, the black drummer, and all subsequent issues carried portraits of musicians. Like Art's bands, the covers were mixed, black musicians scrupulously alternating with whites. The radio program also centered on the musicians. Neither, therefore, took any part in the critical warfare that was tearing the jazz community apart in the forties, until after Art was subjected to what Harriet Choice, the former jazz critic of the* Chicago Tribune, *called "some of the most vicious attacks ever printed about a musician."*

The causes of the jazz wars were complex, but it is surely fair to say that they had their origins in the sheer rapidity of stylistic changes in jazz. From the twenties through the forties there was a new jazz style every decade: traditional jazz in the twenties; swing (primarily a big-band music) in the thirties; and bebop in the forties. Musicians who had learned their trade as young men in the twenties were only in their late thirties and early forties when bebop began in the first half of the 1940s. There was, not surprisingly, a certain amount of hostility among the different generations (if one can apply such a word to a ten-year phenomenon) of jazz musicians. The traditional jazz musicians were contemptuous of many swing bands, seeing their music (not without some justice) as a commercializing of earlier jazz. Both traditional and swing musicians tended to be hostile to bebop, at least when it first appeared. Louis Armstrong called bop "one long search for the right note," and when Dizzy Gillespie was a member of Cab Calloway's brass section, Calloway told him, "Don't play that Chinese music in my band." Swing musicians often thought of traditional jazz as primitive, and bop musicians thought the same of both swing and traditional jazz.

But the hostilities among musicians were by no means universal;
many of them respected their colleagues in other styles. And they were
certainly less intense than the hostilities of the critics, who, with too
few exceptions, spent more energy in denigrating styles they did not like
than in praising those they cared for.
  In those days the critic who was most hostile to traditional jazz was
Leonard Feather.

No one has ever explained why Feather became so incensed at traditional jazz, or should I say traditional jazz musicians. One of the best
of the jazz writers, Ralph Gleason, once expressed it this way: "Jelly
Roll Morton must have kicked Leonard in the ass."

Whatever the cause, the hostility was virulent: some measure of it may
be had from a review of recordings by the rediscovered New Orleans
musicians Bunk Johnson and George Lewis, written by Feather and
Barry Ulanov for the "Two Deuces" column of Metronome *(December*
1943, p. 24), which reads, in part: "The fact is that Bunk and his
cohorts, all old enough to be at least grandfathers . . . are hopelessly
incapable of producing anything that could possibly be called real music,
or real jazz or real anything else except real crap."
  Similar judgments, if that is the word, had been directed at many of
Art's colleagues, but Art himself had escaped them, perhaps because he
was not easily classifiable: he seemed then as now to be first of all a
blues musician, and only second a traditional jazzman. Feather had
seemed to share that view of him in a favorable review of Commodore's
reissue of "Selection from the Gutter," in the September 9, 1943, issue
of Look. *He called it "a sincere and authentic jazz piano solo," and*
referred to Art's "highly distinctive and characteristic blues touches."
Yet in the January 1944 through March 1944 issues of Metronome,
with his colleague, Ulanov, he mounted a critical attack which was as
unrelenting as it was vicious.
  Art has asked himself why. He had apparently made some enemies
through his radio show, in spite of his clear policy of devoting the show
exclusively to small-band jazz, which most stations ignored.

People were always approaching me with records to play. Some wanted
me to plug a record. One bandleader sent me a crate of oranges. As
there was no return address, the Hodes family was on the juice while
it lasted. The only thing I can remember doing that would turn Leonard

Feather around was not playing some early Duke Ellington records for him. At that time Feather was doing public relations work for Ellington. I tried to explain that although I admired Duke I was trying to showcase small-band jazz. I said no. That was one cat that never forgot. I was invited to press parties and backstage warm-ups. But like the ostrich my head was buried in the sand of the one music I loved and wanted to do my all for.

Whatever the motive, the attack began in the January 1944 issue of Metronome, *where the Two Deuces said of two sides recorded by Art's Columbia Quintet, "these sound like an amateur band entertaining in an air raid shelter. Us, we'll face the bombs." In the same issue was an unsigned attack on* The Jazz Record, *which called Art "a minor pianist whose small keyboard talent has been blown up into a ridiculously large reputation by jazz collectors," and added that "If this were a civilization that rewards mediocrity . . . Art Hodes would be a millionaire." In the February issue, Ulanov reviewed a Town Hall concert, reporting that "Art Hodes presented a pathetic set of piano blues, tinkly, faltering, vapid. Hodes' empty treble trills and skeletal bass made listening to his* Boogie Woogie *and* Barrelhouse Blues *really a chore," and later referred to "Hodes' clodhopper piano."*

In the March issue, the Two Deuces reviewed four of Art's solo recordings, calling him "a well-meaning guy but an inferior musician" and "an outdated survival of a bygone era." They asserted that "nobody who knows music thoroughly, and has worked with him and listened to him at length, takes Art seriously as a pianist. There are literally thousands of young unknowns who could play more real jazz in four bars than Art plays on all these four sides. Even one of the Two Deuces, a mediocre amateur pianist himself [Feather], is willing to take Art on and cut him at any session." And they concluded that "Hodes, we think, is the worst musician who has ever attained such stature in the jazz world."

Metronome had been receiving objections to the violence and un-fairness of their criticism from a few of their readers. Ulanov replied to one of them with some windy self-justifications in the April issue. That issue also carried a brief notice stating that "Art Hodes, pianist, taking umbrage at some critical remarks in METRONOME, *which he charged added up to defamation of character, sued the magazine last month for heavy damages." After that the attacks tailed off. In the May issue the*

*Two Deuces reviewed two of Art's solo sides, grumbling that "both
. . . might well have been recorded back in the Paramount label era [that
is, the twenties]." In the October issue they reviewed four band and
two trio sides but said nothing about Art except that on one side "Hodes
contributes a better organized solo than usual." In the December issue,
George T. Simon (who had taken no part in* Metronome's *assault on
Art), in reviewing an Eddie Condon concert at Carnegie Hall, referred
to "some piano by Art Hodes, whose taste and touch impressed me
more than they ever had before."*

So far as Art was concerned, the war with Metronome *was over. He
had sued for $100,000, but he and his lawyer had settled out of court
for costs (which were substantial) plus a subscription to* The Jazz Record.
*The subscription, Art says, never arrived. No other musician had been
subjected to so sustained an attack, but many had received their share
of critical venom. At least two of them, and one of their friends, took
it even less well than Art. As Carlton Brown reported in "The Battle of
Jazz" (*Pic*, January 1946, p. 70), Feather was "knocked down on at
least three separate occasions [and] clipped again on the rebound."*

*Critical abuse of the sort I have been quoting, no matter how clearly
it may seem to be motivated by animus, is never good for a performer
in the short run. The chief damage Art remembers, and regrets, was the
loss of a prospective recording date with Lester Young, the greatest tenor
saxophonist of the swing period, and a man much admired by bop
musicians. One of the jazz recording companies had the provocative
idea of coupling the two because, although they were associated with
very different band styles, their individual styles were solidly based in
the blues. But the date had fallen through when* Metronome *began to
give Art such an ugly press. "It wouldn't pay me now to do it," Art
was told, "with all the critical unacclaim you're getting."*

*That was a major loss, of course, for jazz lovers as well as for Art.
In the long run, however, the jazz wars did him no other lasting harm,
and his entry into broadcasting and editing had done him a lot of good.*

I'd been gathering an audience, and I started runnin' jam sessions in
the Village, at La Casita. Well, one of the jam sessions I ran, I hired
the great Sidney Bechet. I don't know what happened to Sidney the
night I hired him, but he didn't show up. And didn't call up. So I ran
around the Village and got somebody to sit in for him. The Village.
Just walk down the block and around the corner and you were bound

to run into someone you know. Condon had an apartment there. Pee Wee Russell, Muggsy Spanier, Rod Cless, you name 'em. Julius's Bar, right smack kitty corner from Nick's—our hangout, a place to see just about anyone. I used to say, "That's where I get my mail."

I forget who I got, but I got somebody. I promised the disappointed fans that next time I would have two clarinet players to make up for it. I got Rod Cless and Pee Wee Russell. So naturally the next time was the time that Sidney came. Now I got three. Well, I was pretty headstrong in those days, and I didn't feel good about that nonsense. I just let him blow all night. When the night was over I wouldn't pay him. Boy, he was in a stew. He was goin' to Harlem to get his knife and come back and take care of me. George Brunis went with him, to talk him out of it. Well, I was adamant; I wouldn't pay him. In fact I turned my back on him when he got real hot.

A few days later I get a call from an executive on the trial board of our union. He says, "What's this I hear about you not paying Bechet?" So I told him the story. He says, "That's fine. We've been waitin' to nail that son of a bitch for a long time. This is just fine. Let him come up here, and you come up here, tell your story, and we'll finally nail him."

Well, that I didn't want. Here was a guy whose playing I really respected. It was one thing not payin' him. It was another thing us appearing against each other at the union over a measly eight or ten dollars. So I wrote out a check and sent Sidney his money. It was probably one of the best things I've ever done, because from then on there was nothin' he couldn't do for me. We had become friends. And I think Sidney done me so much good I could never recount it.

Art would continue to sponsor jam sessions throughout his stay in New York, sometimes on his own and sometimes in collaboration with Rudi Blesh, the jazz writer. And in spite of the loss of the recording date with Lester Young he recorded prolifically: for Decca, Black and White, Session, and Jazzology; for World Transcriptions and the Voice of America; for his own Jazz Record label; and above all for Blue Note. The last-named firm, owned by two refugees from Hitler's Germany, Francis Wolff and Alfred Lion, was one of the two most important jazz record companies at that time, the other being Milt Gabler's Commodore.

The recording dates for Session (which was owned by Phil Feather-ingill, Metronome's Chicago Editor) and the first two Blue Note dates were in March of 1944, when Metronome's *attack on Art was at its worst. Clearly, neither label's owners took it seriously; indeed, the first side cut for Session was an original composition entitled "Feather's Lament." Art made eight sides for Blue Note on his first two dates, and that was the beginning of a five-year relationship in which he was virtually a staff musician for them, acting as leader on many dates and as sideman on others. The last was cut on March 23, 1949, less than a year before Art returned to Chicago.*

Beginning in 1947, Blue Note would devote itself increasingly to bop, but in 1944

they were puttin' out trad jazz. Dan Qualey, the Solo Art guy, was the one that introduced me to Wolff and Lion. We were friendly. They came to hear me, and things like that, till they finally got this idea of makin' a record date. Of course I jumped at it. I was delighted.

Relations between Lion and Wolff and the musicians they recorded were easy and informal. They would meet with the leader of the date, pick the sidemen first, and then the tunes, always picking a few extra in case some of those they had scheduled didn't work out. If any of the tunes might be unfamiliar the leader would work out a skeletal chart. At the studio

they always came with a bag full of the finest sandwiches you could buy—whatever you wanted—corned beef, roast beef, pickles, soft drinks. There was always a taste for those who liked to indulge. So they were very nice about it, and there was nobody in the studio but the band. They always sat behind the glass window, except Wolff was allowed to roam and take pictures. But he was kind of unobtrusive. He didn't bother us, not at all.

Many of the Blue Note sessions were with Sidney Bechet.

When Blue Note called me to do a recording date with Bechet he was anxious and glad to do it. Knowing Sidney, that would have never happened if I hadn't healed that breach. And although I was the leader on the date Sidney knocked himself out on the session, making it good.

Wild Bill Davison, cornet; Pops Foster, bass; Fred Moore, drums; Sidney on soprano; and myself, piano. We'd rehearsed, practiced, worked out arrangements. Now it's cuttin' time. Should be no problems, right? Wrong. We're not gettin' in there. That rhythm is not tight, the way it should be. But we're in the middle of a number, and Bechet is taking his chorus. You stop the band? Not Sidney. While taking his chorus, improvising, Bechet would lean on a note with a bit more emphasis, almost like adding a push and a pull, bending the rhythm section to his will, working it in line, helping to warm it up. He was making us come alive. And all the time Bechet is soloing, putting down his best on shellac for all time. This was the first time this ever happened to me. Bechet was one great swinger.

We must have cut at least two dozen records together. We were coleaders of many a Blue Note date; either I was the leader or he was the leader. He acted the same on all of them. Bechet not only played for himself and for his audience, he played for the band. On a record date, Sidney was like a band after they'd been blowing two hours. He got there warmed up. I remember Wingy Manone doing that. He'd take the band somewhere, some place we could blow, and we'd play right up to the minute it got feeling real good. Then Wingy would say, "All right, let's go." And off to the studio. Maybe this is New Orleans style. I don't know. I know it worked. After the date Bechet and I would sit and listen, play it back. It had to be good or we'd do it over.

When we made the "Weary Way Blues" [with two clarinets and rhythm], and we needed Albert Nicholas, I went to Bechet's house and rehearsed. I played the second part, the part Albert would have to play, while Bechet played his part. And after I got it just the way he wanted it, I will never forget him saying to me, "Now go over to Albert and teach that little boy his part." Which I did.

In the forties the Negro performers hadn't reached that high place in the sun they now occupy. So "the people" didn't look too kindly on a Negro giving work to a white player when his own people were so in need. I don't think Sidney ever gave that second thoughts. Like the date we cut where the drummer didn't suit Sidney. Next date? A new drummer. The drummer he parted with was colored. The one he hired was white. It didn't matter to Sidney what or who you were. All you had to be was a producer. Music was his business. He didn't mix music with politics, economics, race.

10

52nd Street and the Village

There were many jazz clubs in New York in the forties, and Art worked in most of the best-known places, beginning with Jimmy Ryan's, on 52nd Street.

There was once a street. What a street! Don't look now; it's gone. But it was there. For me it started when you hit the corner at Sixth Avenue: the White Rose. Only we, the musicians who play it hot, cool, every-which-way, called it the One Rose. A saloon where we stop for that opening and closing drink as well as for the few or many we may find we need that night to get through it safely. All of us who worked the street would hit there before going on and during breaks. It was our meeting hall. You like to run into any and everyone. Step up to the bar and have a few goodies and you were ready for the evening. Yeh! And that bar believed in giving you that extra-large taste. Plus you got to chit-chat with your brother musicians.

On the street places come and go; almost every club had several changes of name. As you turn the corner you see a long line of old four-story houses, mostly furnished rooms. The first club you hit is the Three Deuces. After that it's the Downbeat, the Spotlight, and finally the Keyboard. Across the street on the corner, within a great big fenced-off cemented lot, the Douglas Aircraft people have on exhibition a great four-motor job. One of those planes of tomorrow. For two bits you can climb up and stare, and the visitors really do. A couple of doors past is the Onyx Club and then comes Ryan's. That's it. Swing Street.

Pick any kind of music you want to hear. Go from one club to the next. Coleman Hawkins, Barney Bigard, Billie Holiday, Red Allen; the revered names were all checked in on the street. Every club has its doorman, who, on Saturday night, turns out to be the barker. "Step right in, folks; the show starts right away. Hear the world's greatest jazz singer, Billie Holiday." Those guys hustle trade. It reminds you of the circus.

For me it was Jimmy Ryan's. Ryan usually featured a trio during the week. On Sundays Milt Gabler and Eddie Condon took over and it was a jam session at five. You likely to run into the best in the land, all working for a big fat ten-spot. Most of us blew at least half that just being in the room. A long store-front room, not too wide, with the bandstand at the far end. Packed! Ryan's at most contained 110, 120 people, and that wasn't lawful. They'd squeeze in, at a buck a head. Sometimes the promoters broke even. Nothin' fancy, but if you ever got invited to play that session, you'd arrived. And don't think you could just walk in and say, "I got the next chorus." You waited. And you waited. Finally, you were asked to make the scene.

Whether you play or not, you're there. Everybody you knew attended. It was our Sunday-go-to-meeting gathering. Piano, bass, drums would single; all the rest you'd have two, three of every instrument represented. Jack Bland, Eddie Condon; Kaminsky, Marty Marsala, Lips Page; Brunis, Sandy Williams, J. C. Higginbotham; Bechet, Pee Wee and Rod Cless. And always the last number of the session would floor me. "Bugle Call Rag." And after a gang of calls the group would hit that next part. We called it "Ole Miss." That's where the individual choruses would flow. And someone would work out some background riff and you knew you were in the right place 'cause it was mellow.

I still remember an afternoon that some trumpet blower was having lip trouble, complaining about the horn and mouthpiece he had to blow on, and Eddie Condon remarking, "Man, if Bix was here he'd just pick up that horn and blow; he'd blow anybody's horn." And the time when Mezz Mezzrow was hitting one note, high and continuous, and Red McKenzie said, "I thought somebody got run over by a streetcar." And the scene where Bechet was up front, leadin' the front line, and the drummer took a long, extended solo and got himself all twisted up and out of time. Afterwards the house came down for his performance. I don't know what it is about people. They just love to hear drums take off—good, bad, or indifferent. Just the idea that he's working. Bechet got that cat out in front of Ryan's and chewed his ass off. You see, it didn't matter how loud they clapped; you had to make it with the musicians.

Jimmy was always around, greeting, talking to the people. A warm personality. At one time he'd been a Broadway-show bit player. It was his brother-in-law who set up and conducted the business. I finally hung in there long enough to get the trio job. I had me Mezz Mezzrow on clarinet and Danny Alvin, drums. That was a good trio. Danny played it all the way with a beat. Mezz was a blower. The blues was Mezz's bag; that's what turned him on. And he felt the blues. So he didn't run the instrument like the New Orleans greats. You could say he was a clarinet player of few notes. It was a simple kind of playing, but he'd blow at you, and with intensity.

That trio worked Ryan's twice: in the spring of 1940 and in the fall of 1944. One evening during the second gig

the trio got to sounding so good to Jimmy Ryan that he offered to buy us a drink. Now Danny and I would indulge, and we were known to buy our own on occasion. Mezz went the dry route unless he was offered a drink. So Alvin and I ordered our usual. Not Mezz. "Give me three-star Hennessey." You have to remember that this was the war years, and many brands of liquor were scarce, especially brandy. But Jimmy had invited us. So down the cellar he went and got that rare bottle, opened it, and poured. I don't have to tell you one sips brandy. Not Mezz, he tossed his down in one gulp. Ryan just stared. Then he said, "That's like feeding cream to a pig."

Mezz had enough ego for any three people. Some customer dropped in to say that "Barney Bigard is next door sittin' in with Benny Goodman." Mezz heard what the man said, and, without the slightest sign of a smile, turned to us and said, "Man, I think I'll go in there and blow 'em both out of the room."

Mezz was working for me when he and Bernie Wolfe got busy on his book, *Really the Blues*. When it hit the press I read it through. In fact I was so engrossed that I never put it down till I'd finished it, even when I knew it was in part fictional. Certainly when it's mentioned that Mezz made arrangements for Louis Armstrong we all drew a laugh. Among us jazz players "arrangements" was just another word for marijuana, and Mezz was king of the hill when it came to the best in town. When anyone said "the Mezz" we knew it was the best available. When you got a stick it had to be like the thickness of your little finger, and great.

But the Mezz shouldn't be written off. He fought for the jazz he believed in, fought for it when the warriors were few. Mezz was an organizer. He had one of the first mixed bands, not because he was tryin' to prove something, just because he loved it. He lived black. Mezz forsook Chicago long before I made the move, moved to Harlem, and in time married a Negro woman. Mezz went all out when it came to loving "the people" and the music. When he was busted (the law put him away on Rikers Island for selling pot) he made a point of insisting he was black: "Put me in with the colored guys." Mezzrow came on strong, but he lived with his convictions, and that at a time when it wasn't popular.

I was to work Ryan's three or four times as leader. I played there with several trios. I had another trio there in 1948 with Cecil Scott on sax and clarinet, and Baby Dodds playin' the drums. And Chippie Hill was singin' with us. What a beautiful blues singer she was. She'd go out to the end of the room and start from there, singing. No mike. And by the time she hit the bandstand she'd have gathered her children in; that whole audience was like in the palm of her hand. And Cecil could charm her. When she came to work she could be in a mood, but Cecil would look at her and then say, "Chippie, where did you get that hat; you look beautiful." And she'd wilt, and beam, and we'd be together. Those were the beautiful people.

Cecil Scott. Here's a guy operating on one leg, one of the warmest people I knew. His smile was contagious. Always jolly and passing it on. Someone told me Cecil had lost his leg jumpin' out of a window to escape an irate husband who had put in an unexpected appearance. It could be just a story; when I knew him he had settled down. I'll never forget the day Baby Dodds and I visited Cecil at his home in Harlem. He had a railroad flat, a first-floor apartment with a long hallway running through the length of the apartment. Cecil took us into the kitchen for a taste, then called in the family. He had eleven children, from the baby to the oldest, going on seventeen. I had to ask, "Man, how do you guys operate?" To which he answered, "We eat in shifts and we sleep in tiers." And the spirit of that home — unbelievable. Pupils running in and out all day. Plus a few cats and a dog. Life all around him. When we had our third child, Cecil sent his oldest daughter over to my home to take care of things while my wife was recuperating. No question of money: an act of friendship.

If ever there was a guy that impressed me, that I really dug, it was Cecil Scott. He could blow. Play his clarinet sweet for you or dirty. Then there was a way of playing it that would make me think of someone talking to a chicken. Cecil knew all about that. It was later that I learned that the recording by Clarence Williams I'd been enjoying for years, especially because of the clarinet playing, was something Cecil had done: "You're Bound to Look Like a Monkey When You Grow Old." No, you didn't wait for Cecil Scott to tell you what he'd done and where he'd been. You discovered it later in small talk with others, or reading in music magazines.

One scene keeps comin' back. I'd gone out to Harlem to do a benefit with Scott and others. It was a warm affair, and I partook of the goodies. In fact I overpartook. Now we had to get to our gig, Ryan's. I drove and Cecil sat beside me. Central Park West. The snow had fallen. It seemed bouncy, beautiful, with lights flashing on. Most enjoyable. Even sirens. Eventually I got the message and stopped; the lights and sirens were the po-lice. I was more than numb; I was in a cast. Immobile. So the man with one leg had to get out of the car and talk to the cops. Cecil's humor, the nice way about the guy, got across. I got off with a lecture: "Drive slowly, park the car, and go to work." You know I'll never forget Cecil.

Another man Art won't forget is Nick Rongetti, who ran the oldest jazz club in the Village.

Nick's gone, and so is the place, but it sure blazed while it ran. Nick was a pianist turned nite-club owner, and he certainly knew his jazz music and musicians. The players he employed looked like a *Who's Who*. Pay? Well, so-so. But it was the spot to play, and even if you weren't working there you'd drop in and give a listen. During the years that no other spot in this country featured jazz, Nick did. There were times when he couldn't meet his payroll. That was when he could have changed his policy, maybe featured mickey-mouse music, or girlie acts, or any of a dozen different ideas that were thrown at him. Only he didn't.

Which brings to mind the night a famous swing(?) vocalist was visiting the bistro and suddenly broke into song. Nick jumped up like he'd been shot. "What's going on here, anyway?" he asked. Somebody told him the great honor that was being paid him. Nick shouted, "I don't care who he is; if he wants to sing let him go outside." And that was that. Yes, the man Rongetti was stuck on our kind of music. Stuck on it and by it. Nick's face would light up whenever that music was in there.

I never met a cafe owner who did as much for jazz as Nick did. And I'd like to lay you a bet that there were certain musicians that were helped more by Nick than they were by their family or closest friends. But the big thing that he did was that he founded a home for jazz music during the dark ages, the lean years. When I reached New York City in '38 one of my most immediate problems was to find a place to sit in and play. At that time the Spirits of Rhythm were holding down the intermission job at Nick's. I managed to sit in one time and after that I was set. But not solid, man. I had to fight for that seat. You see Nick loved to play piano, and every chance he could steal from his business, he did. He really got a kick out of playing. Still, he never turned me down when I asked if I could sit in. Never.

Nick was an imbiber. He came on strong. At 9 P.M., when you started playing, Nick was reaching a 1 A.M. tempo. I remember this night I'd decided to stay straight till about midnight. You know, kind of feel my way into the evening. Only I never got away with it. Nick expected you to "Come on," as Mezz would say, "with the come on." After that first set I felt so brought down it took a few to bring me around. Nick never said anything to me. But you felt it. You see, he felt it; he lived it.

Then there was Max Gordon and the Village Vanguard.

Max Gordon, a little guy, but big. An eye for talent. A basement club with a tight room. More than a hundred people was not unlawful, it was a menace. Low lights; atmosphere. The Vanguard had a folk-jazz policy. The folk part was featured on the floor; they were starred. The jazz players, mostly trios, played for the acts and played for dancing or just listening. I always enjoyed working there. Burl Ives worked there quite often and when he didn't he used to come in just as often, and eat. And that man could put it away. Richard Dyer Bennett was another regular. Max also dug calypso performers — the Lion of Trinidad, who used to sing "Always Marry a Woman Uglier than You," 'cause a pretty woman will give you nothing but trouble. Pearl Bailey, Leadbelly, Eddie Heywood, Jr., Zutty Singleton. He had 'em.

Zutty Singleton, ace drummer man. I got to tell you about Zutty having the trio at the Vanguard. He had a good trio, but one night he came to work feelin' no pain. He got on a kick to hear himself. So he tells his piano and clarinet men, "Lay out; I got the next choruses." And he proceeds to play solo drums for more than fifteen minutes, sittin' there smiling to himself. Had his own world going. He was a big man. Called everybody "Face." One time I asked him about it; here's how he got to using that term. Fate Marable was top dog on the riverboats, had the best band and the best job. Someone brought Zutty over to introduce him to Fate, who was looking for a drummer. Singleton, young and a bit rash, stepped up and stuck his hand out with a "Glad to know you, Pops." Marable stepped back a pace and spoke: "Face, don't come so close to me—your breath." And for days after that Zutty was going around asking friends, "How's my breath?"

The first time I worked for Mr. Gordon I had Max Kaminsky on trumpet and Freddie Moore, drums. At that time Kaminsky was just out of the armed forces, and I remember he never indulged on the job, but afterwards he'd have to have a bottle just so he could get to sleep. That war period shot his nerves to hell. Freddie Moore had worked with King Oliver, had good credentials plus a good beat. It was at the Village Vanguard that I got Freddie to make up some words for my tune, "Blues and Booze":

> Baby, baby, baby, what makes you snore so loud?
> Baby, baby, baby, what makes you snore so loud?
> You may be a little woman,
>   but you sound just like a great big crowd.

All the time those eyes were rolling. Funny cat.

I found out he'd played washboard, way back. So I got him to bring it down, but he needed thimbles. Now it was wartime, and metal was hard to find. My dad solved it; being a tinsmith, he made a set for Freddie. Was he ever proud of them! It was really somethin' to hear Moore take off on that washboard; he made beats like a dancer.

The next time the Vanguard hired me to bring in a trio I used Wild Bill Davison with Freddie. Big Bill Broonzy was the feature in the show, playing guitar, accompanying his own singing, and that made it for me. He came from an era and a school where you had to do it for yourself, no props or echo chambers, sometimes no mike. If it rang out you rung it, like when piano players used both hands. So Big Bill would step out on that floor, and like Chippie Hill could hold you, just he and his guitar. Ever hear his

> If you white, you aw-rite;
> If you brown, stick aroun';
> But if you black, get back, way back.

You missed it.

This was a big man, over six feet. Big hands. A real kind person. When he talked to you, he kind of bent his head. I never heard any harsh sounds come out of him, in conversation or music. And what a pleasant guy to be around; a guy you could be around without too much talking. But don't chip in for a jug with him. Wild Bill and I did that one night. I was low man on the totem pole, and after Big Bill lowered that fifth the waters had receded below that big hand. All I could see was depreciation. The time you spend with a guy, it's gone, and he's gone. But you remember. He carried no visible scars. Oh, he felt it, and he wrote it. But then he sang it out. A big man, Bill Broonzy.

11

The Living Is Never Easy

One of the odder places Art played was the Stuyvesant Casino, a Jewish catering hall on the lower East Side. One of his bands followed the Bunk Johnson band, the group of New Orleans veterans whose rediscovery was one of the major jazz events of the forties, after their first engagement there.

Bunk Johnson, the last link between the past and the present. Bunk Johnson, who'd worked alongside the legendary Buddy Bolden. Bunk, who'd influenced Louis Armstrong. Of course I'd been hearing about this, because I was very close to the scene. Someone had given *Jazz Record* a picture of Bunk that he had sent to a young fan. There was a note attached that read, "Just a few lines to let you know that I am feeling a lot better at this present time. . . . Now I did enjoy your very fine letter that you wrote me, and it made me feel about thirty years younger, when I was in my prime and could really make a band go, but . . . now I have gotten to be an old man, but I can yet play a mean trumpet." When Bunk wrote that he went on to say that "the 27th of December I passed my 63rd year; now I was born December the 27th, 1879, so you know I have been here a long long time." We published that in April 1943. It took almost three more years before the Bunk Johnson band opened in New York City.

The place itself was a big nothing, but it could (and did) hold some 1600 people. There were long tables, the kind you see at picnics. No fancy stuff, plain wood. Just get your pitcher of beer and put it down. The promoters were to get the admissions; the income from drinks went to the house. Prices were reasonable. You could dance if you cared to, and Bunk encouraged dancing. Certainly the tempos he played were meant to be danced to. The floor was usually full up. The bandstand was about three feet above floor level. A great big old-fashioned upright piano stood at one end. I doubt it had seen a good tuning in years. There was a balcony that stood way back, back end of the dance floor, and that became my listening post for many a night.

I get a kick out of how these New Orleans bands set up—drums at one end, piano at the other, band in between. That's the way Baby and Johnny Dodds set up at Kelly's Stables, back in Chicago [in the twenties]. But this band had a sound of its own. I'd never heard any music quite like it before. Bunk, trumpet. George Lewis, clarinet— sings it right out. Jim Robinson, trombone—loved the bottom land, laid that gutty sound in there for the trumpet and clarinet to operate in. Jim didn't waste musical words, nor did he possess an overabundance. His musical vocabulary was short and to the point. Alton Purnell, piano, doing his share. Marrero, banjo. I'm not a banjo fan, but this man fit the band. Slow Drag, the bass player, a person aglow. Baby Dodds on drums, added attraction.

Jazz music as it was before it got a musical college education, folk jazz. The front line were more rough than polished. As individuals you could pick 'em up and lay 'em down, meaning they didn't make me forget their contemporaries. But together, that was another thing. The band swung. They had a style that was fresh. Take this one tune, "Tiger Rag." We'd been playing it for years, usually hot and fast. Not so the Bunk Johnson band. They played it like you would a fox-trot. And no one, least of all the dancers, was exhausted by the end of the rendition. Fact was, there'd be so much applause that it called for an encore. And you know what? This was somethin' new for me, they turned around and played the same number over again. And nobody, nobody, left the floor.

The band sat; every one of them sat. When they took a chorus the featured player stood up, but mostly they played sittin' down. Some tunes were arranged like I'd never heard them played before, and that was standard New Orleans arrangements, like "Panama." It had several parts we Chicago and New York musicians never played, and they were damn interesting. Like, why hadn't we been playing it that way? Bunk would stand up, up front, and knock off the tempos with his foot. And when the band was ready to go out—finish the number—Bunk would again hit his foot on the floor, and that was a signal they all recognized.

Another difference between this band and the bands I'd had some part of was the amount of ensemble playing that went on. There was a whole lot of playing by all the band before a chorus was turned over to the first soloist. Even then, he was backed by the other two horns for at least part of his performance. This band was a whole new ballgame. I was impressed, enthralled. I never sat in but once. It was happy birthday night—could have been Bunk's. Red Allen was there. Big Bill Broonzy and Leadbelly did a duet on "The Saints." But aside from that occasion I had no desire to experiment. This band was a together thing, with a sound all its own. No one should change that sound by sitting in.

I never did find out who did the PR work for the Bunk Johnson troop, but whoever it was did a bang-up job, for the major mags— _Time, Life_, etc.—and newspapers gave this venture great coverage. It all centered on Bunk, the trumpet player out of New Orleans who was the link between the legendary Buddy Bolden and Louis Armstrong. For the most part little was said about the sidemen. Bunk was the idol, and from what I could see he played the part to the hilt. He milked it. He had his adorers wait on him and serve him: "If you're goin' out, pick me up a couple of silk shirts, size so-and-so."

Bunk was natural. He'd sleep right on the bandstand, in front of everybody, in the same chair he'd been blowin' in, band playing away. Someone called Wild Bill Davison to rush over and sub. Bill doesn't blow soft. Bunk just slept through the rest of the evening. It was somethin' to see. He was a great one for sleep. One night I caught him sittin' up front listening to Red Allen's band, one of the loudest groups I've ever encountered. They blew up a storm. Bunk was sittin' right in their collective lap, asleep. Man, I don't know what he had goin', but if he could have bottled that? Wow!

Bunk Johnson. Like the song says, he's been here and gone. Tough man. They're all gone. You should have heard Bunk whistle his chorus on down, then pick up his horn and play the same bit on out. You know there are lots of people who play music but can't play by hear. Yeah, I said by hear. I mean it's doubtful if they're hearing it coming out, or even before. Bunk heard his music. It sang out of him, from inside out. All he had to do was put the horn to his mouth. The stuff was there. I know, there's more to it than that—you have to be able to play the horn. But please, not if you're speechless.

A lot of yesterday's jazz can stand up and be counted right now, today. We're likely to forget that. You hardly hear any of it, except on occasion, like when company comes, and you drag old gramp out, dressed up. So you ask, "What was gramp like?" He was quite a man, one hell of a blowing man. You need never be ashamed of him. He certainly enriched many of us.

The band had an apartment, more like a flat, and it was like New Orleans in New York City. That band was just about sufficient unto itself. Like one guy could cut hair and did, so no need for one of them to wander outside. And he didn't. Same with meals, red beans and rice. My mouth waters when I think of good New Orleans cooking; I've eaten it. So that was a plus, but in such close quarters you have to come up with minus, especially with Bunk absorbing all that adoration. It was a wonder they lasted as long as they did.

Gene Williams was the one who approached me. "Art, would you like to bring a band into the Stuyvesant Casino?" That's the first I knew that it was over, and I was sorry to see it happen, as much as I dug gettin' the job. No problem, I had the band. I had Kaiser Marshall [and, later, Baby Dodds], drums; Cecil Scott, clarinet; Henry Goodwin on trumpet and Pops Foster on bass; George Lugg on trombone—he was white. Another one of my great mixed bands, four colored and two white, one of the best bands I ever had. It was a happy band; we loved being together. I think we were at the Casino for about sixteen weeks. From the Casino we wound up going to the Ole South. And, like all bands, eventually we disbanded.

The night they closed at the Ole South Art took the band to play a concert at Penn State, with Sidney Bechet added as a guest star. Art played a lot of college concerts in those days, but the Penn State one stands out, partly because State College, Pennsylvania, was even more inaccessible in those days before superhighways than it is today, and partly because that was the trip on which Pops Foster lost his teeth.

Two college men drove down, waited till we finished work, helped us pack. We didn't get away till close to 6 A.M. I remember Sidney and I riding together. I don't remember the rest of the seating arrangement except that Baby and Pops wound up in the same car. It was a long trip. We slept; we napped. For a while we carried on conversations, but mostly we cooled it. When we finally got there it was out of the car and get some rest in the rooms that had been arranged for us.

When the other car arrived it didn't take an expert to see that Baby Dodds and Pops Foster were feelin' no pain. Somehow there was a jug in that car, maybe more than one. They were stoned. In a cast.

Fractured. Here we were, with a concert in a few hours and my back line out of it.

It was Sidney who got busy. You got to know Bechet. Any time he works with you he treats the job exactly as if it was his own. He insisted on both the culprits taking a cold tub bath, soaking in it. After that aspirins and black coffee. And finally he got both of them to dress and walked them to and fro and around the block. He gave them no rest; no sleepin' it off. Concert time came and they were both in action; a bit cute at times, but they played the gig and played it well. At one point Pops balanced his bass on one foot, and while still playing walked around. Of course he brought the house down. Baby, not to be outdone, walked all over the stage, playing with his drum sticks on anything that would respond. The crowd loved it.

Bechet and I just fell out on some couch afterwards. Eventually Pops, Sidney, and I boarded a bus for New York City. The other three stayed over. I found out, days later, they got involved in some town nearby, trying to solve the colored question between drinks. It took days for them to return. Sidney and I continued to catch up on sleep as the bus chugged along, but Pops wasn't ready to give it up. He found some sailor, and a bottle appeared, and I'm sure the long trip home was shortened considerably.

We arrived, collected our baggage, and met bus-side. I got the payroll out and counted out Bechet's money. Then I began counting Pops's money, and he counted with me. Sidney interrupted: "You ol' son of a bitch, what did you do with your teeth?" It seemed that Foster had misplaced a set of uppers. It wasn't hard to reconstruct the scene. As Pops continued to drink his teeth became heavier, so he must have taken them out and laid them down on the bus seat. But by now the bus, which let us out on 34th Street, had gone on its way. So we three raced down to the bus station at 42nd Street. But search as we did, we couldn't come up with Pops's teeth. It seemed obvious that some joker had picked them up for laughs. Finally we went our separate ways home.

That's how Art remembers it. Pops, in his own autobiography, says he lost his teeth at Penn State instead of on the bus: "I got so drunk I dropped them in the toilet and flushed them down before I knew what happened." Nineteen years later Art had Pops flown to Chicago, from San Francisco, to play a TV date. They hadn't seen each other in over

fifteen years. "We went through that date like we'd never been apart,"
says Art. They traded stories. Pops reminded Art of a date they'd played
when Art got so drunk he couldn't stand up, and Pops had propped
him up against a snowbank to cool off, and then forgotten him until
after the concert. "I knowed you wouldn't freeze," said Pops, "you had
so much antifreeze in you." And Art responded with "Pops, what did
you tell your wife when you got home from that Penn State gig without
your teeth?"

So that was an odd job. But the oddest job Art ever played was in
the summer of 1947, at Camp Unity, in Wingdale, New York.

I had Henry Goodwin on trumpet, and I had Kaiser Marshall and Cecil
Scott. I had Herb Ward, a white bass player. Sandy Williams, the
trombone player, he was my roommate. Camp Unity was a labor
camp—a camp for laboring people. A cheap vacation. That's all I knew
about it when I took the job.

But it didn't take long after his arrival for Art to discover that Camp
Unity was run by the Communist Party. The American left was interested
in jazz at that time for ideological reasons; jazz was, as the subtitle of
a forties book put it, "A People's Music." The Party was split, like
apolitical jazz fans, over what sort of jazz one should like: traditional
jazz (because it came from the folk) or bebop (because it was progressive).
Art's employers must have belonged to the first group, and they may
also have liked his having a mixed band.

But Art and the Party didn't get along. One source of friction was
their censoring the tunes he played. They wouldn't let him play "Dear
Old Southland." "Well," says Art, "I guess I can understand why they
wouldn't like "Dear Old Southland." But they also wouldn't let him
play "Summertime." "What's wrong with 'Summertime'?" Art asked.
They said the lyrics were offensive. "We don't sing the lyrics," said Art.
The lyrics were still offensive, even unsung. "What's wrong with the
lyrics?" Art wanted to know. "They say 'the living is easy,'" was the
answer. "The living is never easy."

The food at Camp Unity was good, and plentiful, but tasteless. "That's
the first experience I had," says Art, "with people wrecking good food."
And the indoctrination was constant. They wanted him to take classes
in economics. He responded by asking them for a raise. They invaded
the band room, and were shocked to find the musicians shooting craps.

My band room was my castle. Don't tell me what to do in my home.

They tried to. They says, "Why don't you play chess, instead?" I says, "I don't dig chess." And they didn't understand me, you know.

Someone asked him what he did in the winter time.

What does a musician do in the winter time? The same thing he does in the summer time; he plays music, man. So I said, "I wear a coat."

It got so they'd follow me in the men's room, and stand on each side of the urinal, and say, "Why don't you join us?" So between the silly questions and the pursuit to become one of them, I was beginning to feel out of place. And one day they read me off, just as though they were reading me out of their conclave. And there was nothing for me to do but walk out of that job, just pack my bags and go home. I just didn't have no time for that nonsense. Maybe I lost work, but that's the kind of work I can afford to lose.

Before he finally left New York, Art had one of his best jobs, in a little room he ran himself, along with Pee Wee Russell. It began when Pee Wee and Art, who were both out of work,

walked from 52nd Street to the Village. We weren't athletic, just broke. And as we neared the Village Pee Wee said, "You know, I know a man who's got a club, a little spot on the corner. I don't think he's doing anything with his back room." I says, "Well, lets go and talk to this cat—see what he says." The place was on Seventh Avenue, almost kitty-corner from Nick's. It was called the Riviera. We went in and saw this boss, Joe, and he was real nice, and yeah, he knew Pee Wee. He took us in his back room. He says, "Look, I'm not doin' anything with it. If you fellas want it, go ahead." So we're goin' to open up a back room. And actually, what do you call it? You call it Pee Wee and Art's back room. And the man put up a poster outside.

Now mind you, neither Pee Wee or I have got a dime. We haven't got dime one. Joe saw our problem and offered to staff our venture. There was a piano in the room; all we needed was a waiter, because the front part, which contained the bar, also served our room. Actually, we needed more than that; the least we could get by with was a trio, so we hired Herb Ward to play the string bass. We promised him seventy-five a week.

We still don't have a dime, but one thing we did have was friends. Eddie Condon had a club a couple of blocks away. Television was just comin' in then, the tail end of the forties, and Eddie had a show of his own. Of course Eddie really dug Pee Wee. So he gave us a date on television, and they built a set for us, and they called it "Pee Wee and Art's Back Room," and let us play a couple of numbers. Eddie loaned us George Wettling on drums. The publicity was going out; we were in business. Our boss Joe gave us another boost, advanced each of us thirty dollars so we could survive the week. And he kept that up for many a week, in my case increasing it weekly as we went along.

At this time, 1949, Art was in better physical shape than he'd been in for many years. Like most jazz musicians he had been a heavy drinker, and like most jazz musicians had experimented with various other drugs. "I never got too hooked on bennies," he says, "but one of my friends got so stoned using bennies he ground his teeth down. Fact." The drinking had become especially self-destructive, and Art had made up his mind to break with it. "I got off everything in 1948," he says. One of his compositions, "Blues Keep Calling," is both a commemoration of that decision and a reinforcement of it:

> Now night has fallen,
> > darkness settles down on me,
> And blues keep calling,
> > calling everywhere I see,
> Gotta get myself together,
> > bottom ain't no place for me.

But while Art was healthy

Pee Wee wasn't in the greatest health. Having to drink was like medicinal. We worked around it. Instead of him standing up when we played I suggested that he make the rounds, sit with people and carry his clarinet, and play as he felt it. Our audience liked that. That place was so small there'd be togetherness; we wouldn't be that far apart. And then Pee Wee would stroll over to the piano and finish the set. There was always somebody falling in and wanting to play, so the job was never a hardship.

Well, pretty soon people started discovering this little room in the Village, where occupancy by more than ninety people was not only unlawful, it was dangerous. I still remember Phil Harris comin' in, and borrowing a pair of sticks somewhere, and just sittin' at the table and beatin' away. At the end of the first week we instituted a policy of inviting the musicians to drop in on Friday. That seemed to be a good night. And they would drop in and blow and stay all night—buy their own drinks. One fellow that did a lot for me—I never will forget him—a very warm character, beautiful player, drunk or sober a gentleman, and a real performer—Hot Lips Page. Another trumpet player that supported us was Red Allen.

Tony Parenti came in one time and Barney Bigard was blowing with us. He was playin' a long blues. I remember Jack Teagarden just standin' there, not even blowin', just standin' there listening to Barney. There was nothin' else to do, it was comin' out so beautiful. After that blues somebody says, "Play 'High Society.' " Well, that's Tony Parenti's tune, not that he wrote it, but it's the kind of thing he would do well. There's a traditional chorus that New Orleans clarinets usually play. We had three clarinets—Pee Wee, Tony, Barney—tackling that chorus. Pee Wee played it like Thelonious Monk would tackle "Sweet Georgia Brown." No way would he depart from his style—it came out "Low Society." Barney started playin' that traditional part, but when Tony picked up his clarinet and joined in Barney started playin' harmony to that chorus, like a third apart. It's one of the hardest things I can conceive of a man doin', a harmony part so true I fell out, and Tony was just flabbergasted. That's one time someone should have had a tape recorder going.

About this time we decided we needed another man, to play intermission piano. We were fortunate; Willie "the Lion" Smith was available. That's like finding diamonds in your dresser. I remember having Barney Bigard on a TV show in Chicago, years later, in which he says to me, "Man, I used to love to come in and hear you and Willie bump heads." What he meant, of course, was that I'd have to go on after Willie played. And anybody that follows Willie—well in the first place, you'd better have better sense, because Willie's a giant. He really could play. He played a lot like Fats, struttin', like. Stride. Put a cigar in his mouth, and anytime he'd play he'd make throat noises that came out, "Hoomph, hoomph, hoomph." I suppose that's why he got that nickname, although I never asked him. He'd "Hoomph" all the time. Always carried a cane, and to hear him sing, "I Wish I Could Shimmy Like My Sister Kate"—in Yiddish, yet! Seems that Willie had been raised either by or around a Jewish family.

There was a little boy came in—well, he was about twenty or so, but he liked to play the trumpet. I won't mention him by name, but he was pretty sad. You know how Willie handled him? He wouldn't run him off. He'd take out a coin, a quarter, and say, "Here, boy, go get me a cigar." Needless to say, Willie was out of cigars all night. But the boy learned a lot sittin' next to Willie—learned how to play in more than just one key. Willie was great for teaching and patience. And talk about an appetite—I've only seen one man eat like Willie, and none of 'em drink like Willie and eat. I seen Burl Ives put away a steak and then call for an encore—same large steak. Well, Willie could put away a pound of hamburger and after that a half a fried chicken. Wash it down with brandy and a beer chaser, and no problem for the Lion to consume a dozen such drinks within a few hours. But if I was waiting for this to affect his piano playing I had a long wait a-coming.

One night Chippie Hill dropped in for a visit—Bertha "Chippie" Hill. Chippie had been a line girl, a chorus girl, when the late Bessie Smith was singin' in clubs, and Bertha heard her. She had her own style, but you could tell something of Bessie's had rubbed off on her. Man, that was an experience, hearing Chippie sing. I can shut my eyes and see and hear Chippie shoutin' a song right now. She'd stand in the doorway which separated the back room from the front room, and she'd sing her blues, or shout, and hold both audiences in the palm of her hand. The boss hired her right on the spot. I wish you could have heard her and Willie. The Lion would vamp on the keys, all the time carrying on a conversation with Chippie, sort of, "Chippie, do you remember?" She would answer and he would keep it goin'; they could do a half-hour easy without so much as going into a song. They'd break me up.

Now the joint was really jumpin'. We had talent comin' out of our ears. Pee Wee wasn't as good to himself as he deserved, but he didn't cheat others. He gave fully of what he had. Ever see some of the faces he'd make when he chorused? A woman in labor couldn't emote any better. Some of the most touching bits he's put together came through at such times. Pee Wee was inspired. But you can't be inspired every night, and Pee Wee, of course, during this time wasn't in the best of health, and we rested him a lot.

One time while we were there we all got a rest. Louis Armstrong was takin' about a week to have his teeth fixed, so his whole band was out of work, and the boss thought, wouldn't it be a good idea if we got Jack Teagarden in here. And we agreed, even though it meant we would be out of work. Well, Jack was there about a week. I think he had a new clarinet player every day, even to sending to Philadelphia for a clarinet player. I don't know why he had trouble with clarinets. I don't think Jack drew any money. Every night he'd take home half a dozen bottles of one thing or another. Of course there was always people around Jack. As I said, Nick's was right across the street, and Jack would get through playin' one set at the Riviera. Then he'd go across and play a set with the band at Nick's.

That job, that back room, ran from about January to January for me. One night I got a call from my agent, Freddie Williamson, asking me if I'd like to take an all-star band into the Blue Note, in Chicago. Well, the bread was so good—twice what I was drawing at the Riviera—I had to think, and I found out that Pee Wee would go with me. Freddie Moore said he'd go, and Chippie Hill said she'd go. So in January 1950 I bid New York goodbye and went back to Chicago.

12

Goin' to Chicago

When Art went back to Chicago, he knew he'd be playing opposite touring bands at the Blue Note, Chicago's best-known jazz club, and Fred Williamson, his agent, had hinted at much more: "Art, this could turn into something big, and you can stay at the Blue Note until the band's ready." At that time Williamson was working out of the Chicago office of Joe Glaser's booking agency.

Early in January 1950 I was back in Chicago, the city I'd despaired of some dozen years ago. I brought Pee Wee, Fred Moore, and Chippie Hill with me. In Chicago we were joined by trumpet man Lee Collins and trombonist Floyd O'Brien. On paper it figured to be a good band. And with Chippie doing the down-home vocals ("If I can't sell it, I'll keep sittin' on it") we had to be an attraction. Frank Holzfeind, the manager, played name groups opposite us, so the burden of packing the joint wasn't our baby. It was great and it was comfortable.

One day Fred called me into his office and unfolded his plan. What he wanted to do was build an all-star group, the Dixielanders, that could hit the road and play just about every spot Louis Armstrong played. The clout would be "If you want Louis then take the Dixielanders." The next time around we wouldn't need that help; we could make it on our own.

As Williamson was Joe Glaser's man, and Joe was Armstrong's mentor, the deal looked kosher. But it came as a big surprise to me. The plan was to hire George Brunis, trombone, and Zutty Singleton, drums. It meant parting almost immediately with Floyd O'Brien and Freddy Moore, my friends of long standing. That would be the first move. After they had settled in we would get Wild Bill Davison to replace Lee Collins, bring in Pops Foster on bass, and Sidney Bechet would join us as an added attraction. With that line-up, both Williamson and

Frank Holzfeind felt the Dixielanders couldn't miss. It certainly looked great on paper.

The day arrived when Zutty, George, Pee Wee, and I reunioned. I had met Zutty at the train. Took him to my quarters and we broke bread. Drove him and his drums to the Blue Note. It was like old-home week. Zutty had been my mentor in past years and he'd helped make my Decca recording successful. Brunis and I went back to our coleader gig at Childs. Brunis and Singleton went way back to their days in New Orleans. "We the People," as Brunis referred to Pee Wee, was everybody's favorite. It was a festive evening. Five bottles—two fifths and three pints—went down the drain in less than six hours, and I wasn't drinkin'. It looked like we were off to a great start.

The Blue Note policy certainly made the job bearable. We could be assured of a good house when Erroll Garner or Sarah Vaughan played the club. Now let me tell you somethin' about Sarah Vaughan. When she arrived on the scene, Chippie had to give up her dressing room to Miss V. That didn't sit well. It never openly flared but you could feel it in the air. But after Chippie went up to sing, and Sarah heard her, from then on it was Miss Vaughan who would make the introduction about Miss C. and actually lead her up on the stage. She was showing the people how she felt about Chippie's talent. It really impressed me.

But the Blue Note band never jelled.

Looking back, I can see that the Blue Note was a once-in-a-lifetime shot, and we blew it, collectively. We never got further than the band as it then stood. We talked to Wild Bill about joining us, and he would have. He asked for $275 a week. That was $100 more than our guys were getting. I was getting $50 a week extra to pay the union and have someone take care of the government tab; the fellows knew and no point was ever made about it. But you should have heard the screams when it was suggested, "Let's get him (Wild Bill); after we get started and the money starts rolling in we'll equalize things. No one will lose a dime over it." All to no avail. "He's no better than I am." "He won't draw any more people than I do." Etc., etc. . . . There was no changing that thinking.

Professional jealousies were just one problem, drinking was another. Sometimes there were more bottles on stage than musicians. And when George Brunis had been drinking, which was often, it wasn't easy to get him off the stage. He would head for the piano and sing an endless series of songs he had written. One of them consisted of a list of the common accusations against Eddie Condon, set to the tune of "Mother":

C is for the con he hands the people.
O is for the old routines he plays.
N is for the new fad he's created.
D is for the dough he never pays.
O is for the old friends he's forgotten.
N is for he never plays guitar.
Put them all together, they spell CONDON,
The sweetheart of the D.A.R.

It was funny the first time you heard it, especially if you knew that the last line referred to the D.A.R.'s refusal to rent Constitution Hall, in Washington, D.C., to so raucous a group as Eddie Condon's jazz band. Condon rented the Willard Hotel ballroom instead. In any case, Brunis's act could be tiresome. Art remembers one of his first performances at the Blue Note.

We had finished our set and Frank Holzfeind had announced, "And now Miss Sarah Vaughan." We had all left the stage, all but Brunis, who had suddenly felt the urge to go into his act. This took him to the piano where he sat down and went into a routine best known as "Then I wrote." One wag I knew called it the Turkish Hit Parade. Meanwhile Sarah Vaughan was waiting to go on. A house full—over a hundred people—were waiting to hear her. Brunis was just getting warmed up. Now it was Holzfeind's turn to get into the act. He kneeled at the far corner of the stage, where he couldn't be seen by the audience, and beckoned to George, called him. "Georgie!" Undaunted, Brunis went on and on. If it wasn't so serious it could have been funny. The only solution finally hit Frank. He shut off the microphone. That brought awareness, and Brunis left the stage.

Many times Holzfeind and Williamson sat with me and impressed on me the need to "beat Brunis to the mike." That also was funny. The mike stood center stage and within arm's reach of George; I was some six feet away. Occasionally, when George wasn't aware, I'd get there first. It must have been a scene from up front. One customer confided in me, "I'm not spending ninety cents a drink to hear that bum." And really, I would talk to George. Pee Wee would talk to him too. George was very agreeable; he'd nod. We never had harsh words.

But the act never changed. Add to that Pee Wee getting sicker and sicker. We wound up having to hospitalize him.

Even Art's not drinking was a problem.

The tight feeling I had always had with Zutty disappeared almost immediately. I have to share the blame there. I'd sobered up since we last played music together, and frankly, after you've been high playing music, it's not quite the same being off the stuff. In fact it took me a long time before I felt at ease operating without imbibing. So I'm sure my timing was off, and Zutty's tolerance just wasn't. Well, we were making it, but not much more than that. We managed to hang on for eleven weeks.

When the band broke up, Chippie went back to Harlem, where she met with the cab accident that ended her life. The burial was in Chicago.

She was laid out in a parlor on the South Side. Tell you one thing about my colored brothers. They know how to conduct a send-off. You get all the cryin' done, and over with. Jimmy and Mama Yancey, Johnny Schenk and I commiserated, knowing we were heavy losers. She was one of a kind. Pee Wee wound up in San Francisco and almost didn't make it, that time. But he did recover. I don't know whether Singleton went east or west; eventually he and Pee Wee both wound up in New York. Brunis stayed in Chicago and I decided to give it a try. The town had changed enough so that I could have a mixed band, and there seemed to be work. The union hadn't changed, but you can't ask for everything.

Why stay in Chicago instead of heading back to New York? Art liked the slower pace.

Two pictures come to mind that explain my inner feelings. The first occurred when I was new to New York. I had to catch a subway train to Grand Central and then shuttle over to the East Side. As I started toward the shuttle train a bell rang. Immediately all the people started running to get into that train before whoever was just inside that door got shoved in and the door closed. I started running like the rest of them. And all the time I was in New York the rush was on. It was move it or lose it.

The second picture is from much later, in the seventies, when Art and producer Bob Kaiser of WTTW brought Bud Freeman out from New York to do a TV show.

A few local players who knew Bud from way back—Bud came out of the Chicago scene in the twenties—called me and asked me to talk to Bud about sticking around a few days. They'd get together a party and just enjoy seeing and being with him again. So I broached the subject to Freeman, and I'll never forget his answer: "Art, I'd love to, but I've got to get back to New York. My phone is ringing."

Art liked Chicago's pace for his family, as well.

Family had become important to me. I dug my wife, Thelma, and we had three offspring at that time: Janet, Bob, and Karen. Plus my father was living with us. Add to that, my wife was pregnant and expecting any minute. During my stay at the Blue Note we were in constant telephone communication. The gist of the conversations was, "If Chicago is it, find us a place to live." The only other family we had was settled in Chicago. Thelma's sister Pat was married to an entertaining pianist, a piano-bar pianist, Chuck Wright, a damn good performer. Actually I was staying with Pat and Chuck during the whole time I played the Blue Note. I had two sisters in the Windy City; they liked the idea of us moving back. So the search was on. I just didn't have any luck until I saw the ad in the paper about a new town, Park Forest, some thirty-two miles south of Chicago. Anyway, I went out there. Lots of mud and unpaved sidewalks, but it was new and clean and available. By May 1st, 1950, we were in our new home, once again together as a family. Park Forest has been home for us ever since. It's comfortable. Middle-class.

At first they rented. It's very difficult for a jazz musician to buy a house, because it's difficult to get a mortgage; moneylenders don't look kindly on people who can't say where or whether they'll be working next year. But eventually Art was introduced to one of the developers of Park Forest, a jazz fan of many years standing, who was delighted to find so eminent a musician living in his community. "But," he asked, "what are you doing in the rentals?" Art explained; a mortgage was arranged; and the Hodes family were able to buy a home.

From that time on Art has worked out of Chicago: worked in Chicago itself when there was a club for him to work in, and gone on the road when there wasn't. His first job after the Blue Note was a two-week

*booking as a solo at the Dome, a hoodlum-run club in downtown
Minneapolis, the first of many bookings in that city. It went well, except
that*

after every set the owner would be on the platform rearranging the
microphones. It seemed he couldn't hear me. After three nights of this
I finally asked him, "Who did I follow in here?" When he said "Red
Allen" I understood. No way in the world could I produce the sound
that six-piece band did. Man, they could wake the dead.

*As Art settled in to Chicago, he made up his mind to set limits to
the road trips. He would gladly do a week or two in another city. He
would even do one-nighters, but not all year long. That decision came
after thinking over a challenging and flattering offer.*

On three different occasions feelers came my way regarding me joining
Louie Armstrong's All-Stars. Barney Bigard was the one who really
wanted me in that band. He told me several times, "You belong here;
it's your gig." The thing was, the All-Stars only came to Chicago every
two to three years. No family stays together apart. Barrett Deems, the
All-Stars drummer, told me his daughter didn't know him when he
came to Chicago. She ran away from him—climbed a tree. So, much
as I would have given to play with that band, I had to walk away.

A great symphony orchestra is able to work in their home town,
but not a great jazz band. To the very last, Armstrong had to hit the
road constantly in order to ply his trade. Ellington the same. Think
of it. Both around seventy, still having to make the road scene. Same
thing going on with the Count—Basie. By this time in their lives we
should have been going to hear and see them.

*Even in New York in the forties, in the years of the great jazz clubs,
Art, like most jazz musicians, had to spend some of his time out of
town: a couple of weeks or more in Philadelphia, or Haverhill, Mas-
sachusetts, or Columbus, Ohio. And he played dozens of one-night or
one-day gigs at Eastern schools and colleges, along with the one-night
jam sessions he often sponsored. But after the two-week solo gig in
Minneapolis his new manager, John Schenck, found him a job that kept
him in Chicago from June 1950 to July 1951. It was at Rupneck's, a
club at 5900 North and Broadway.*

It was a six-piece band: clarinetist Jimmy Granato, who had played
in Jimmy Durante's jazz band; Floyd O'Brien, trombone; Jimmy Ille,

a cornet player; Bill Moore, bass; and Bill Pfeiffer on drums. The band clicked from the very beginning. It had spirit and it had musicianship.

The nucleus of that band — Art and Jimmy Granato — played together, with occasional breaks, until 1958, and the band retained its character through many changes in the rest of the lineup: Whitey Myrick on trumpet, for example, and Muggsy Dawson on cornet; Al Jenkins and Danny Williams on trombone; Kenny White and Earl Murphy on bass; Buddy Smith and Hap Gormley on drums. Buddy was a link to both the founding generation of jazz and to bop: his uncle, who had taught him drums, was Andrew Hilaire, the drummer on Jelly Roll Morton's classic Red Hot Peppers recordings, and Buddy had played with Charlie Parker.

After Rupneck's they hit the road.

We played St. Louis, Toronto, Milwaukee, Denver, Detroit, St. Paul. Even played a gambling club in East Cape Girardeau. Let me tell you about that last gig. The room we played in was very comfortable except it had no people; we were playing to empty tables and chairs. The boss told me not to worry but to keep playing "inspired." It turned out that the customers were in another room, gambling, and they could hear us. But what a queer kick, playing for people you can't see.

In Denver the owner, Bob Cummings, was a jazz lover; he knew what he was buying. He booked Louis Armstrong and other jazz groups. But the sleeping quarters weren't adequate. Two people would have to share a room, and in one case two had to share the same bed. Little Muggsy Dawson had to sleep with Granato. As Muggsy explained it, "I got nothing against Jimmy. But when he inhales the mattress rises, and when he exhales it sinks. I'm waking up sea sick."

Two gigs were memorable because of a happening they shared. We'd arrived in East St. Louis and set up the band. Meanwhile I'm looking for the boss, the cat who had signed my contract. I wanted to check in. I was told don't worry about it; everything's aw-rite. Just go ahead and play. Which we did. But I couldn't connect up with the boss, which had me nervous. I needn't have been; at the week end I got my salary. Some three days later I discovered where my boss had been. They found him in the trunk of a car, disposed of. Business goin' on as usual, though.

Then in Milwaukee I ran into a real pain-in-the-ass of a boss. True, business wasn't happening, and that makes for unhappiness. But that's happened before; why make the job miserable? This time I had a real hassle gettin' my bread and gettin' out of Milwaukee. Like I had to make a federal case out of it, and hang around and hang around before the bartender got the OK, over the phone, to pay me. Some days later one of the guys in the band showed me a picture in the newspaper. After being missing for a few days our boss had been found, well shot up, in a car. Another trunk job.

The fifties wasn't all road gigs. There was often work in Chicago: a stint as house pianist at Jazz Ltd. in 1953, for example, and band gigs at Helsing's, the Blue Note, the Capitol Lounge, and the Silver Palm, among others. There were two lengthy bookings at the Brass Rail, the first of them running from July through November 1955. Fred Smith, an agent, got Art an audition there, and the audition got him the job. The Brass Rail was as colorful a place, in its own way, as the Liberty Inn, and the boss was as colorful in his way as the McGoverns.

Louie—I never did get his last name—has to be in a class by himself. One night I happened to look down at the bar as an Italian came in, stocky, somewhere in his thirties, from the old country. I saw him lay down a bill. He got his drink and the bartender returned with his change. The Italian picked up his money, started counting it, and got mad. In broken English he shouted that he'd been cheated, and he started banging on the bar with his fist, looking for attention. And he got it. The bartender grabbed the banging hand. He started to bang with his other hand; someone reached over from behind and grabbed that arm. Talk about frustrated. He almost sputtered, "I'm gonna call the cops." With that, Louie stepped in and whacked the poor soul a few good ones in the pit of the stomach. "Cops, you want? Go call 'em." And with that he threw the Italian out the door. Louie came back talkin' to himself. "Cops! Let 'im call 'em. I'm paying 500 of 'em; let 'em earn deir money."

Louie wasn't lying. He was a contributor. Once a week a police sergeant followed Louie into the men's room. He carried a bag—the bagman in action.

On niteclub gigs, come the end of the week you look to get paid. As that first Saturday night rolled into the A.M., I scanned the house. No boss. So I asked the second in command, Benny. A bit later Louie came in and got the message that I had asked about pay day. Next thing I knew he was climbing the steps that led to the stage and me.

He slapped down a stack of bills on the piano keys. No question, he was mad. Well, I had a set to finish. We did. Then I stepped down and started counting out the money, and something was wrong. Definitely wrong. So I counted it out again. The third time I started counting Louie came over, grabbed the money out of my hands, and counted it. "What the hell's the matter with you, Benny? Can't you count? There's a hundred and forty dollars too much here."

Let me tell you, if I'd 'a' kept that money I'd 'a' been in big trouble. But that action on my part led to an understanding between us. I was there to play music—to the best of our collective abilities—and to observe certain unwritten laws that went with the job, like don't mess with the gals who worked there. Louie was tight on that. From then on I never wondered when I'd get paid. It was always there, on time.

No question about the respect the help had for Louie. He was the boss and they were in his corner. There was always a number of gals that worked the place, "B" girls. It wasn't unusual to see a lone man come in, order a drink, then hear the bartender tell him, "That'll be five dollars." The buyer would erupt, "What, for one drink?" And the bartender would tell him, "These two gals are having one with you." And sure enough, there were two pretty young ladies, one on either side of him, lifting a glass and looking at him with a "Here goes." Usually, after one drink, it was here goes as far as the buyer was concerned. But the Brass Rail was at Randolph and Dearborn, a populated area. We'd get all sorts of people in and out of the joint all night. Like a downtown barber shop, they didn't figure you as a steady customer. So get it while you can.

Those gals were there strictly for business. One night a kid I knew from south suburbia dropped in. When I first saw him he was sitting in a booth with one of the hostesses and they were having a taste. The first opportunity I had I took Mark aside. "Man, you're playing a losing game. All you'll wind up with is the morning edition of the *Chicago Tribune*." Well, youth will be served. I talked and Mark nodded, then went on doing just what he'd been doing. The gal he'd been sittin' with came over to me and said, "Art, I know he's a friend of yours, but if I don't take him someone else will." One hundred dollars later my young friend got up and left the place, alone, just as he had entered.

If you had enough scratch, that could get you a seat on the balcony. On one of those slower nights a chap came in and sat at the bar. You wouldn't have noticed the look that passed between the bartender, who had sized up the customer, and someone in the rear of the room. That started the action. A good-looking hostess joined him. "How about me having a bottle of wine with you?" It sounds innocent enough. What appears is a coke-bottle size of domestic champagne. That cost you twelve-fifty. How can you refuse after you said "OK" to the bartender? Then you look the gal over and there goes one more.

After that the gal got as friendly as the bar permitted. These gals had routines. Blew in your ear or ran her hand over your thigh, once lightly. Enough that when she said, "How 'bout you and I having our drinks upstairs, where we can be alone?" the warmed-up soul responded positively. Once they were in a quiet corner where they seemed unobserved the gal got amorous: kissing on the neck, and tongue in the ear. Got the man excited so when she switched to a bottle of wine in the bucket of ice there were no "Noes".

That bucket technique was somethin' else. The waiter appears and fixes the champagne bottle into the bucket. A few minutes and he's back, opening the bottle. Now he pours each a drink and retires. The gal picks up her drink and toasts her "love." As she starts to drink she pauses, leans forward to kiss her man, and pours most of her drink into the bucket over the sponsor's shoulder. You go through a goodly number of champagne bottles that way, and it don't take too long. That waiter is up and down like a yo-yo. It's twenty-five bucks a throw, plus something for the waiter. Meanwhile our hero is getting everything but a physical. And the guy was always led to believe there would be a later. Never happened. In this case, four hundred bucks later it was over. Home, James.

Louie had friends all over the place. One night he gets a call from a club down the block that a guy was headed our way and was loaded. The minute he hits the door one of the special dollies has him, and a few drinks later he's in the dice game. Who should be in the game also but Louie. It seemed like good old times from the sounds coming from that turf. That is, for a few hours. Soon it was over, and our main attraction left. Within minutes the attractive hostess took a duck, and shortly after the police arrived. It seemed someone had dropped a bundle at the Rail. Would you believe a guy could drop six grand in a twenty-six game? Simple dice game. Usually you roll the house for drinks; anything else is illegal.

No one knew a thing. Louie was gone. So was the hostess, so there was no one to identify. And though the loser lodged complaints at the police station, nothing happened. No, I shouldn't say that. Money did change hands. And the pretty hostess, who was a blond, went on vacation for several weeks. When she reappeared we had a redhead.

The day came when I was offered a part in a Broadway play, titled *Jazz Getaway*. A speaking part. I was gonna take the whole band with me. The producer was a tight friend and we had many a talk session together. I got good local publicity, and Louie was really proud of this. He was so glad to see me get this break. One night, arriving at work, I see this great huge cake, at least two feet high, built up like they do wedding cakes. It's right in front of the bandstand, and it spells out "Good Luck, Art" and more such words. It was from Louie, of course. I'm tellin' you I was touched. That turned out to be the only highlight of my big show-biz deal. I was available and ready, but main characters continued to come up missing, and eventually the backers came up missing. And so did the production. *Jazz Getaway* never got away.

After the play folded, Art's band had its second run at the Brass Rail, from February through September 1956, with some weeks off in the summer, when they backed Connee Boswell at the Blue Note as well as playing on the road. When they finally left,

the Brass Rail went on, and played people like Jack Teagarden, Joe Venuti, Wingy Manone. Louie kept listenin' to Fred Smith and Fred kept asking me for advice. When you hired such names, in the fifties, you were hiring the best in trad jazz. I don't know if Louie realized it, but he was helping to keep the music alive. He was one of the few. I couldn't tell you what happened, but the day came when the place folded.

13

Scuffling

*Jobs for jazz musicians—especially for traditional jazz musicians—
were getting scarcer all through the fifties. Rock was becoming the music
of young Americans, who had always before provided much of the
audience for jazz. Television was becoming a national addiction. Club
owners were discovering that canned music was cheaper than live musicians. And one by one the musicians themselves were leaving full-time
music, or leaving jazz for Mickey Mouse music. But Art had made a
permanent commitment when he first gave up regular pay checks for
jazz, back in the twenties. He stuck with an increasingly difficult business.*

*He did another stint as house pianist at Jazz Limited, a club that
for more than twenty-five years provided a home for traditional jazz in
Chicago. It was run by a clarinetist, Bill Reinhardt, and his wife, Ruth.*

It was on Grand Avenue, near State Street, just north of the Loop. A
small club, seating capacity close to 100 if you pack sardines. Bandstand
in the back. A small service bar in front where two or three could sit.

When Ruth and Bill opened the club in the late forties they imported
the likes of Big Sid Catlett, Muggsy Spanier, Doc Evans, Joe Sullivan,
Brunis. The jazz names played the spot. Someone once asked Big Sid
why he would play a joint like Jazz Ltd., and Sid promptly answered,
"It's not a joint. When Big Sid plays there it's *the* spot in town." That's
what made Jazz Ltd.: the music, the players. As Ruth Reinhardt once
remarked, and later had printed on table cards, "If you want to dance,
go to the Aragon Ballroom. If you want to drink, try any bar. You can
make love in a taxi. But if you want to hear Dixieland, this is the
place." Or some such words. I have no script; I'm remembering.

The club was Ruth's baby, all the way. Mrs. R. knew the ropes.
She'd been a line girl in a Billy Rose production in New York. A young

Eurasian chick had fallen in love with a tall American clarinetist. At Jazz Ltd. she'd enthroned her Bill—always the act of deference towards him. Ruth kept an eagle eye on all proceedings. And she could smell trouble a mile away. One evening a party of fifteen came in. Business was slow, but when voices were raised and things looked out of hand Ruth called the waiter and had him hand the party their check. "I know," I overheard her say, "the place will look empty without them. But when people come in after we've cleared them out, they won't be run out by this quarrelsome group." Let me tell you, not many owners would think that through and act on it the way she did.

You had to give Ruth credit. If she needed the cops she paid them right on the spot, instead of weekly. And Chicago is a cop-ridden town. From its very inception Ruth decided there would no hanky-panky at Jazz Ltd. No unescorted women were allowed. If one of the musicians' wives dropped in for a visit, she sat with Ruth. Any wife, hundreds of miles away, could feel at ease if she knew her husband was at the club.

Ruth remembered faces, names. And she'd hip her husband with "Oh, Bill! You remember Mr. Johnson?" And of course William remembered. Made for good business. Ruth had the ability to get people from all over the country to drop in when they were in town. She always seemed to get the convention people; Jazz Ltd. would be busy on weekdays, just like the hotels. Saturday was a so-so night, usually local trade. And many a holiday you could shoot a cannon off in the joint without disturbing anyone.

Bill was the leader on stage. It was his band. The message came loud and clear, "The musicians may change but the music remains the same." There definitely was a formula. There was room for individual expression, but the tunes in the book were there to stay: Dixieland tunes ("Sensation," "Original Dixieland One-Step") or the kind associated with the Chicago style ("Royal Garden Blues," "I've Found a New Baby"). When I came in I used several solo numbers with the band taking part, arrangements I'd cooked up: "When Jimmy Yancey Was a Young Man," "Grandpa's Spells," "St. Louis Blues."

Playing on the Jazz Ltd. bandstand was serious business. If one of the brass, particularly the trumpet man, missed a note, you'd see Bill put a hand underneath his shirt collar in back and squirm. Music there was a production; it wasn't meant to be fun. Early in my tenure at the Jazz Ltd. piano, I learned that I had to ease tensions that at times were so thick you could cut 'em with a knife.

Reinhardt had a thing about New Orleans drummers. He loved that beat. Some of them stayed on at the club for many a year. Freddy Kohlman, he got to be a fixture. No doubt Bill called the tunes and stamped off the tempos, but after that Kohlman took charge. That tempo had a way of coming around to his thinking, and you weren't goin' to budge it. When I worked there I found that the best way for me was to get on board and ride. That way you avoided arguing where the beat should be and the job rolled easier. But when the late Earl Washington resided at the keyboard strange things were happening. It got so someone put up a sign as you came out of the back room onto the bandstand; it read "Experimental Bandstand." The vibrations must have been heavy.

The times I enjoyed most were when Mike McKendrick used to sing "Closer Walk with Thee." He always touched me with that number. And "Grin and Bear It," Quinn Wilson, the bassist, and Barrett Deems, drums. Barrett was perpetual motion, always into something. He and Quinn did a take-off on Bob Haggart's "Big Noise from Winnetka," only they called it "Little Noise in Cicero." But mostly I enjoyed handling the off-night at the club. I could gather my own cohorts, and Ruth was in charge, so it was a loose evening.

After he left Jazz Ltd., Art took his band back on the road.

In February '57 I hit the Turf Club in Indianapolis, and really thought I'd found myself a town. I never saw anyone do a better job of getting people into a club than the promo man who was handling the Turf Club. He'd written the publicity and put out the ads, of course. But more than that, he'd gone into all sorts of business establishments telling them the story of jazz, how it was Americana and should be supported. Opening night you couldn't get in without waiting. The place was packed, and it continued that way for eleven weeks.

But it was a husband and wife team that operated the club, and they got to fallin' apart. Pretty soon one or the other would be out of the club, and many times both. Absentee management. It took an Act of Congress to get a waitress; they were cabareting at some other table. Then you never knew who was handling the cash register. We were still packin' them in, but the male boss was talking that it cost as much to pay off as he was taking in. I could stay if I would take a salary cut. No way could I see that; I couldn't be convinced I'd done the place anything but good. It was time to go.

Where he went was back on staff for Jazz Ltd. But jobs were really thinning out now, and in 1957 he started filling in by teaching piano at the Park Forest Conservatory, nothing so ambitious as how to play jazz piano, but how to improvise enough to be able to play pop tunes. Or, for a very few students, how to play blues. In July of 1958 he became a full-time staff member at the Conservatory, and when Jay Noel, the man who had brought him there, became manager of a Lyon & Healy piano store, Art began teaching at Lyon & Healy.

But teaching wasn't a solution for him. For one thing, he wouldn't turn down a chance to take a band on the road because he had pupils; he would tell them, "See you in so many weeks." And he found that many of his pupils were there only because their parents wanted them to play the piano. "Many a kid," says Art, "I told, 'Send your mother to me; she's the one who wants the lessons.'" So Art gradually eased out of teaching. He stopped running ads and took only those pupils who sought him out. "Yes, I'll teach you," he says, "but only if it's your desire, not your mother's."

Late in 1959 Art got a call from Bob Scobey, who had brought his West Coast jazz band into a Near North Side club. Scobey needed a piano player; could Art fill in for that weekend? At first Art was hesitant. Scobey's New Orleans Revival style of music was some distance from Art's, and Art had been a leader so long that he wasn't anxious to work for someone else. But he agreed when Scobey said he wanted him "even if you just sit there."

It was something I've never regretted doing. Every one of the band was so nice. Understanding. Even the girl vocalist made me feel wanted. So I wailed, and enjoyed the gig.

Before we parted that weekend I accepted a record date on Victor ("Rompin' 'n' Stompin' "), turned down the piano chair in the band, but accepted a job playing opposite Bob's group with a quartet of my own. For four of the next five years I worked opposite Bob, either as a single or producing a band on his nights off. The guy was good for me. In fact, I'd have to go back to my Wingy Manone days to find any one musician who had been so helpful.

Working in the same room with Bob was a liberal education for me. He admitted he wasn't playing for the small audience, although his book contained such jazz gems as "The Chant," "Black Bottom Stomp," "Sidewalk Blues." It was a fast-moving show, not a set. For at least the first two intermissions Scobey mingled with the customers. He said hello, plus a few words, to approximately 350 people a week. Multiply that by four years and you've got a lot of people in Chicago who "knew" him. With musicians he was generous; he paid them more than they'd earn with any similar group, or earned after they left him. If you had something to say musically, you got your chance, within the confines of the formula he had devised for the band. Scobey died of cancer, and none of us who was near and saw the fight he put up to go on living will forget. He was on that stand blowing with nothing inside but guts.

In the early sixties two old friends of Art's, both major jazz musicians, left full-time music. Barney Bigard, who had played clarinet for Duke Ellington and for Louis Armstrong's All Stars, quit because he simply couldn't find enough work. Jess Stacy quit because he could no longer stand the sleazy piano bars, which were the only places he could work regularly. He took a day job as a mail clerk for Max Factor. He and Art had recommended each other for jobs when they were scuffling in Chicago in the first years of the depression. Now Art wrote in his down beat *column, "Sittin' In," "It's a sad commentary on the music business and the musicians union to see a player of the stature Jess Stacy enjoys having to find his livelihood in the cosmetic business."*

Art has kept on, taking whatever gigs he could find, in Chicago and on the road. And he has continued the career of spokesman for jazz that he had begun in the forties. He wrote a regular column for down beat *throughout the sixties. He wrote for little jazz magazines:* Jazz Report *and* The Second Line. *He wrote for* Esquire *and the* Chicago Tribune *and the* New York Times. *And he found other ways of reaching the public. He spent the academic year of 1963-64 playing high school assemblies for the Wisconsin Bureau of concerts and lectures—eighty-eight high schools in all, and when that was over he played adult education programs in the greater Chicago area.*

A piece he wrote for the Chicago Tribune *brought him to the attention of Bob Kaiser, a producer at WTTW, Chicago's educational television station, and they produced a half-hour show, "Plain Ol' Blues," with Art talking and playing piano—a television version of the program he had developed for schools and adult education groups. It won a Chicago*

Emmy for the 1965-66 season. From 1969 to 1971 they did a series of half-hour shows, each of them featuring one or more major musicians: "the likes of Barney Bigard, Wild Bill Davison, George Brunis, Doc Evans, Pee Wee Russell, Jimmy McPartland, Freeman, Eddie Condon, J. C. Higginbotham." National educational television bought six of them as a series, and they got wide exposure.

The show with Eddie Condon and J. C. Higginbotham was a near disaster. Art had been

looking forward to Eddie giving out with some conversation. After all, he'd contributed so much. But he was in a cast—bombed, fractured. He'd found his brother and they had celebrated. No question of him making with the conversation. The camera man should have gotten an Emmy for showing Eddie without showing enough of him to expose his state of being.

But this was the show that attracted the attention of Columbia Artists. I was called into New York to talk about touring the U.S. with this lineup, doing Community Concerts. This led to a seventeen-week tour with Condon, Bigard, Davison, and Jim Beebe, trombone; Rail Wilson, string bass; and Hillard Brown, drums. The show, as I had laid it out, could have played itself: a fast-paced concert, two hours with a twenty-minute break. Trad-jazz, blues, a minimum of talk. Everywhere we played to packed audiences. Had we tended to business we could have gone on for years. Eventually behavior, or lack of it, caught up with us, and reports came back to the front office. When the tour ended we disbanded.

Next season we had a new lineup. I got Jimmy McPartland, trumpet; Franz Jackson, sax; Volly De Faut, clarinet (who never made the opening night; we did the tour with two players in the front line); Jean Carroll, vocals; Jimmy Johnson, bass; Hillard Brown, drums. Somewhere along the line Jimmy McPartland decided he'd had enough and left us. We finished the tour with greater audience appeal than when we started. Jimmy Johnson told me over and over again, "We don't need any stars; this show plays itself."

The remaining musicians—Art, Franz Jackson, Jimmy Johnson, and Hillard Brown—

continued to tour into 1978 for Columbia Artists. Nowhere did we fail to please. I remember one manager telling us, "I don't expect you to knock 'em dead. The attraction you're filling in for is sick, and you're pulling us out of a hole." It was then Jimmy Johnson spoke up and said, "Mister, don't worry about a thing. We bring happiness." And we went on, and the audience stood to applaud. The manager came backstage beaming.

Art lost his wife, Thelma, to cancer in 1980, and he was still grieving when he was booked as a solo into Hanratty's, a New York piano club, in February 1981. It was his first New York appearance since he had left the city over thirty years before, and he got very good press. John S. Wilson, the jazz critic for the New York Times, *called him "the living summation of a great jazz piano tradition." Whitney Balliett wrote his "Profile" for the* New Yorker, *and was equally complimentary. Art's playing, he wrote,*

> *is filled with the blues. . . . He makes rags and "The Sunny Side of the Street" and "The Battle Hymn of the Republic" and "Ain't She Sweet?" sound like blues. His slow blues are full of evening light, of keening winds, of a sense of endings and departures. They have no self-pity, and they seem to encompass every emotion. His slow blues are unique; in their intensity and depth they surpass those of any other blues pianist. . . .*
>
> *The blues are the simplest of all jazz materials, yet they are the most difficult to play well — slow blues in particular. . . . Great blues solos . . . are seizures: they possess both the player and the listener. When Hodes goes "down" into a slow blues, he takes you with him and you don't get out until the last bar.*

Balliett's tribute was as perceptive as it was eloquent. The critical enthusiasm in New York was echoed by a similar enthusiasm in the Chicago press, and all of this, plus a new agent, helped Art into a twenty-two month solo engagement at the Mayfair-Regent Hotel, at the bottom of Chicago's Gold Coast, with time off for bookings out of town and in Europe. In 1983 he remarried. His wife, Jan (short for Georgeann), is a classical pianist, and the two of them have worked up a series of duets which add a pleasant variety to his performances. Since 1985 most of his Chicago dates have been played with a trio: usually Bobby Lewis on trumpet, cornet, and flugelhorn, and Jerry Coleman on drums.

But increasingly his most satisfying engagements have not been in Chicago, or anywhere else in the United States, but in Europe, where he, like so many other American jazz musicians, has found a better audience than he can find at home. His first trip abroad was in 1970, when he played with Papa Bue's Viking Jazz Band in Denmark. Now he averages two trips abroad a year, sometimes to festivals, in Nice and Edinburgh, but also for tours sponsored by jazz clubs in Germany, Holland, England, Australia, New Zealand, Belgium, Switzerland, and Austria. Art notices especially the differences between European and American young people.

Not too long ago I did a concert with a strong lineup at a neighboring college. I'm well known in this area, but it was disappointing; the crowd was scarce. Less than a week later I appeared in concert at a small town in Germany. There were two thousand young people — teens and twenties — in attendance. And that was in the afternoon. That evening we had an equally large crowd. I keep asking myself why? Is it because Europeans have a love for American jazz and we haven't? It would seem so. They buy the recordings, and when an American jazzman comes to their land, they flock to hear him. Many are well informed of our jazz heritage. The best jazz discographies come from abroad. It's like we have the music and don't value it, and they value it and pursue it.

But there's other reasons. Europeans get out more; they're not glued to the tube yet. They haven't all bought the idea that the top ten is all there is to music. And they don't applaud for no reason; you have to get to 'em. Honestly, they make you feel it's all worthwhile. You look forward to going there and playing for those people. By far the best audiences I've performed for in recent years have been European audiences.

14

Hot Man, II

*Art has continued to record prolifically, for Mercury and—with the
Bob Scobey band—for Victor among the majors, and for many of the
independent jazz labels: for Jazzology/G.H.B., which has become a
major label for traditional jazz; for Delmark, which has an impressive
blues catalog; for Euphonic, Paramount, Dotted Eighth, Audiophile,
Storyville, Sackville, Muse, and Parkwood. For that part of the American
audience that values jazz, he is a famous man. When his daughter Karen
went with her high school class on a field trip to Washington, D.C., she
found his picture at the Smithsonian Institution, on the wall of the
room devoted to jazz. But his audience is smaller than that of any
number of second-rate rock musicians. That's nothing new, of course.
In the twenties, thirties, and forties jazzmen didn't have the mass audience that followed any number of second-rate popular musicians. Still,
there are times when the shabby bad taste of the American music business
troubles him. "You can't tell me," he once wrote of another musician,
"that it doesn't take something out of you to know how good you are
compared to somebody else, and see them get the rewards."*

*For the most part, though, he has made his peace with the audience
as well as with himself. He made it when he first decided to play hot,
rather than sweet. He has held almost religiously to that decision, although there were many times when choosing to play hot cost him
something. Back when he started playing hot the choices were clear.
"You could work in Mickey Mouse bands for money and play for kicks
after work at some pub, or you could play for kicks and tighten your
belt."*

*Art played for kicks and tightened his belt. And he has not only
avoided sweet bands, but also big bands. It's not that he dislikes all big
bands; he admires and has learned from Ellington and Basie. And he*

liked playing with the Floyd Towne band, which had trumpet, three reeds, and rhythm. "It was big enough to give you that full sound, when you wanted it," he says, "but not so big it restricted you." Most jazz musicians have preferred small bands to big ones, either because they disliked the restrictions of section work, or because they disliked the streak of commercialism to be found in most big-band jazz.

Art's first unpleasant experience with big bands came early in his career. He was playing with the Doc Rudder band—trumpet, trombone, three saxes, and rhythm—when the management decided to replace Rudder with one Henri Lishon.

Henri L. called a rehearsal. Mr. L. had his own ideas, his own arrangements and his own tenor saxophonist, who doubled on fiddle, to replace Doc. Mr. Lishon also played the y-o-lin, thereby giving us the added distinction of having a string section. After rehearsing waltzes and sweet tunes till they came out of my ears, I got off my stool, went to the rear of the house and sat down. Mr. L. didn't dare challenge me on that; the house considered me too valuable a piece of property to fire.

I just sat and watched the debacle. When those two fiddles got to playing it sure sounded sad. But I didn't reach bottom till Lishon called out, "Let's try the 'Tiger Rag' arrangement." That was it. He had the whole front line stand up. The tempo he beat off was fast. Everything held together fairly well, even tho the arrangement stunk, until the band came to the final "go" choruses. This was the masterpiece. You know the tune; remember the part that says, "Hold that tiger, Hold that tiger." Well, in this chorus, Henri had the saxes blowing two bars of music and the horns the next two, and what with the brass section pointing their instruments at the sax section for one bar and in the opposite direction the next, and the saxes doing likewise, and the music getting louder and faster and all six of the boys standing up on their chairs in a grand finale gesture, well, I almost fell out of mine in a fit of laughter.

After that the blowup just naturally had to come. We were having a snack together when Mr. Lishon started telling Floyd O'Brien how to play his trombone. That was too much for me. I blew my top. After I got through expressing my views on leaders, and on the violin as an instrument in a dance band, especially a hot band, there was nothin' left for me to do but leave.

But his climactic experience of big bands came much later on, when he refused—dramatically—a chance at the piano chair with Benny Goodman.

I was working—I believe it was called the 5100 Club, and I was real happy with the band, and I really had no eyes to join Benny. Jess Stacy brought this group in to hear me and make a decision whether they wanted me to follow him in the band. The club got very excited. It was a big deal, you know, because Benny Goodman was coming in with John Hammond, and with the girl singer. It wasn't Peggy Lee; it was before her.

They came in like royalty. The waiter preceded them, and sat 'em at a table, and almost fawned on them. You know, everybody was so knocked out by the fact that we got Benny Goodman and John Hammond. Of course Jess was like an old shoe; there was no problem there. I was introduced—reintroduced, 'cause I knew Benny as a kid. We were all introduced, the band and all. And then we were playin' a set. And I happened to be playing a blues number, playing alone, and this girl singer, who I'd hardly met, decided to come up on the stage and sing, while I was playing. And I didn't stop playin' the blues and give her a real opening: you know, "Da da, de da da da—Here, fall in." And she couldn't find her way. She couldn't come in. No way in the world did she know what blues singing was. And finally she got discouraged and went back to the table. And of course that finished me with that offer, because soon after that the royalty got up and walked out.

Jess was kind of embarrassed about this whole thing, because he really wanted me. He felt I was the one to take his place, and he'd been pushing me right along. But me not giving her that opening killed it. I just wasn't gonna let her in. If she was gonna sing the blues, she was gonna come in singin'. It was too important to me, the blues, for me to make a mock thing out of it, playin' for a singer on stage. Just too important. So that was another one I lost gratefully. Looking back I still feel very grateful. And now, of course, looking back and talkin' to Jess, he's so grateful, having gotten out of that too.

Which is to say that the hot men have lived in a very tight musical world, where respect for one's craft has meant everything, and access to that world has not been easy.

When Eddie Condon was on Johnny Carson's show, Carson said to him, "I got a whole big band here. Why can't I just pull out five or six guys. Could you make music with them?" And Eddie said, "Not if they were my brothers." Playing music joyfully, and playing music for money—there's a distinction.

It's a funny thing about this music we play. Say you're black, and the guy sitting next to you, he's dark too. But just to the other side of you sits a white player. Now, you and that white player could have more in common musically than you and your black neighbor. Buddy Smith and I used to talk about this often. He'd say, "If I had a brother, and he couldn't play music, I'd feed him and I'd give him money, but he couldn't play in my band."

Art has valued his tightly knit world, and the people in it. He describes himself as "a collector of people." But the trouble with collecting people is that

you lose them. You lose a Broonzy, a Leadbelly, or a Leroy Carr. You wake up one morning and there's no Pee Wee. No Brunis. And these people are one of a kind. A breed apart. You haven't noticed any Jack Teagardens around; no George Wettlings. Save your eyes; there'll be no other Pee Wees.

And since jazz is an improvised music, when you lose the musicians you lose the music.

I came along in a good time. This was an age when we had each other; it was all happening right around you. We had Bix and Bessie. We had King Oliver and Louis. Earl Hines of the twenties. Pine Top. Fats Waller. James P. Johnson. Worthwhile? Man, how can I think otherwise when I recall the list of characters that enriched me as I trod the path. Just the clarinet players; just one instrument. Rod Cless, Pee Wee Russell, Omer Simeon, Mezzrow, Volly De Faut, Barney Bigard, Cecil Scott, Albert Nicholas. And of course the master soprano-man who also played clarinet, Sidney Bechet.

I can remember, in the forties, walking down 52nd Street and in six different clubs hearing six different sounds emerging. No band sounded like Red Allen's. A Teagarden group was distinctive, as was a Condon group. Or, before that, Jimmie Noone's Apex Club group. Johnny and Baby Dodds. That all was. That was here, and that's gone. The music I grew up on no longer exists except as a now and again occurrence. No way to bring it back. There's a few of us still hanging in there, but not for too long. After that there are the records and the stories. So much of it has been preserved. Never as good as being in the room when it's happening, but the next best thing.

There are lots of stories.

Like the time Joe Venuti put an ad in a Los Angeles paper: "Bass player wanted. Meet me at Hollywood and Vine at noon tomorrow. Bring fiddle and be in tux." Some forty-seven bass players showed up to clog this busy intersection. The cops had to chase 'em off the street. Venuti didn't show but the union rightly guessed who it was and fined Joe the going salary for each man. I asked Joe, "What about it?" He said, "It was worth every dollar."

Joe always sent Wingy Manone (who had one arm) one cuff link for Christmas. Wingy told me, "Man, I've got seventeen cuff links, all different."

There was the time a jazz critic had just published a book, and had stopped into Julius's Bar, across from Nick's. Eddie Condon called to him.

"Come over, I want you to meet somebody. This is Ivan, a famous Russian critic." After a bit the "Russian" says to the American critic, "What instrument do you play?" The critic replies, "Nothing." The "Russian" looks him over carefully. "You write on jazz and you don't play an instrument? In Russia we shoot you."

There is Maxine Sullivan's description of her husband, pianist Cliff Jackson: "You know, Cliff was a man of few words. 'Uh' and 'Huh.' "

There was the time

some people invited George Zack to a party and he came prepared. Time to go home and guests were leaving, but not Zack. He took off his clothes and there he was in pajamas. His overnight bag.

There was the time

George Brunis was rehearsing a band; he was going into the Blue Note. This was in the very early fifties. He picked the men himself and they worked out the routines. Now then, when George isn't working he cools it. He stays cold sober. But on stage he likes a taste. After one set on the job George picked up the mike and started telling the audience, "This is the worst bunch of bums I ever worked with." Sober it didn't sound bad to him. But after a few drinks reality set in and he really heard what he had put together.

Or there was the time Yank Lawson and Billy Butterfield were playing with The World's Greatest Jazz Band,

on an engagement that had come about through the efforts of the local doctor, who thought of himself as a jazz pianist. There was no way to keep him from sittin' in, so the band just shrugged and thought to make the best of it. It turned out worse than had been anticipated. Yank whispered to Butterfield, "That's the worst piano playing I ever heard. Have you ever heard anything this bad?" To which Billy replied, "No." Butterfield was known for terse conversations. Yank then said, "How would you like to have a guy who plays piano like that take out your gall bladder?" To which Billy replied, "He's doing it to me now."

Many of the stories, like most of these, are comic versions of the jazz musicians' abiding sense of living in a world of values different from those of their audience, or their critics, or, for that matter, their bosses, the club owners. There was the time a club owner liked Art but couldn't stand his band. He thought they were too old for show business.

He took me aside one evening and told me, "You ought to get rid of those guys. Look at your trombone player; he wears policeman's shoes. What you need is to get four good-looking boys, and teach 'em. Call yourself 'Big Daddy and the Four Lads.' "

Danny Williams, the trombone player, like the rest of the band, was the best man on his instrument Art could find in Chicago, but the boss couldn't see that. "All he could see," says Art, "was a Vegas act."

But Art is content with his life. He is pleased when audiences applaud, even though "They don't always applaud what knocks me out; they applaud what knocks them out." He values the praise of the better critics: Virgil Thomson, who admired his "elegant piano playing"; John S. Wilson; Whitney Balliett. He values even more the praise of fellow musicians, especially the praise of black pianists: Little Brother Montgomery, who told him, "You're blacker than 90 percent of black piano players"; Horace Silver, who said, "If there was no Art Hodes there'd be no Horace."

But finally, of course, it isn't what anyone says that matters.

This music I grew up with comes to mean everything. You play something and the whole evening suddenly becomes worthwhile, even if you and maybe the player alongside of you are the only ones to dig it. What happened inside of you—how do you measure that?

I've never met a jazz musician who retired. I've met some who were forced into other types of work because they needed the bread or couldn't find steady musical employment. Hillard Brown, drummer, who worked alongside of me for many years, is one of many players who had to find another way to sustain himself. He says, "I've been in a variety of businesses, but I never forsake my music. It's what keeps me alive inside."

I've witnessed people who worked their whole adult lives for a company that kept them living in one area, who, on reaching retirement age, pack it all in, sell the house, and go somewhere far off to live it out. But for the jazz player, places and real estate are not where it's at. When I'm making my music it's beautiful inside. And after all, that's where one really dwells.

Most people have to work. I *play* for a living. I don't intend to quit until my hands quit.

A Note on Recordings

Most of Art's recordings are available at this writing. Jazz records are much less ephemeral than popular records. Their relative stability may be seen in the fact that the technological shift to compact discs, which has very nearly made popular (and even classical) long-playing records a thing of the past, is still in process for jazz recordings. Still, they go out of press with alarming irregularity, and when that happens one can only hope that the better ones will be reissued. And because they do not have a mass audience, they cannot be found in most record stores. If you live in a major city you can find some of them, both in the larger stores and in those specializing in jazz. Otherwise you must depend on mail order. One source is Down Home Music, Inc., 10341 San Pablo Avenue, El Cerrito, CA 94530 (415-525-1494). They publish lists of jazz, blues and gospel, folk, and rock records, and a newsletter about new recordings. Another is *Cadence Magazine* and Record Sales, The Cadence Building, Redwood, NY 13679 (315-287-2852). They offer a sample copy of their magazine, which contains their catalog, for $2.50. Both firms carry a huge stock of domestic and foreign jazz records.

Art's first recordings, with Wingy Manone, are available at this writing in the MCA Jazz Heritage Series (MCA-1350: *The Chicagoans*). Howard Rye, who compiled the discography, points out that "In Europe, a Swedish issue, Classic Jazz Masters CJM31, *Chicago Jazz, Vol. 1,* may still be in catalog." He adds that "The determined purchaser should note that what is unavailable in one country may be easily available in another; all jazz specialist shops of necessity carry large ranges of imported discs, though these usually command a premium price."

Art's sixteen dates for Blue Note, from December 20, 1944, through March 23, 1949, have been reissued in their entirety by Mosaic Records,

35 Melrose Place, Stamford, CT 06092 (203-327-7111). This is a substantial body of music; including alternate takes and unissued titles it comes to ninety-eight cuts. The eleven dates under Art's leadership are in a set of five LPs: *The Complete Art Hodes Blue Note Sessions* (MR5-114). The five dates on which he was a sideman are part of a set of six LPs: *The Complete Blue Note Recordings of Sidney Bechet* (MR6-110). I am especially fond of the *Back Room Boys* session of April 21, 1944, and the trio session of April 6, 1945, in MR5-114, and the Bechet-Nicholas Blue Five date of February 12, 1946, in MR6-110. The *Back Room Boys* session contains an extraordinary blues by Art on piano, with Jimmy Shirley on guitar and Israel Crosby on bass, which was, unaccountably, previously unissued.

Mosaic is currently engaged in the heroic task of reissuing the entire Commodore catalog, in three volumes. The years from 1938 through 1943 are covered in *The Complete Commodore Jazz Recordings, Volume 1* (Mosaic MR23-123), a set of twenty-three LPs. (Because of that size, Mosaic limited the edition to 2500 copies rather than their usual 5000 or 7500, and in June 1990 there were less than 400 copies left. They have probably sold out by now.) This set includes two of Art's finest early piano solos, "A Selection from the Gutter" and "Organ Grinder Blues," from the 1940 Solo Art date described at the beginning of Chapter 8.

Thirteen other titles were cut for Solo Art between August 1939 and March 1940; most of the masters came into Art's hands when Dan Qualey ran out of money and couldn't issue them. Five of them are now available on Jazzology J-82, *The Jazz Record Story, Volume One*, along with a piano solo cut four years later and four cuts by Art's Columbia Quintet. Unfortunately, these last are poorly recorded, but they are the only recordings by that hard-driving band. Two of the piano solos, "Bedrock Blues" and "No Pay Blues," are outstanding.

Jazzology is one of several labels started by George H. Buck, Jr., who has become a major force in traditional jazz records, both through his own recordings and through those acquired from other labels. They are available through record stores, but can also be had at a discount by joining the Collector's Record Club, GHB Jazz Foundation Building, 1206 Decatur Street, New Orleans, LA 70116 (504-525-1776). Art was the pianist on Buck's first LP, recorded in the summer of 1949, and over the years he would make twenty-three more. Particularly notable are Jazzology J-104, *Art Hodes Trio: Apex Blues* (from World Broadcasting System transcriptions), a session by one of the trios Art led at Jimmy Ryan's, with Mezz Mezzrow and Danny Alvin; Jazzology J-46, *Art for Art's Sake* (originally Dotted Eighth DELP-1000), which mixes superior solos ("Someone to Watch over Me" and "Washboard Blues" are outstanding) with trios and cuts by the Jazz Ltd. band; Jazzology J-58, *The Art Hodes Jazz Four plus Two: Home Cookin'*, by the quartet that toured for Columbia Artists, with cornet and trombone added; and Jazzology JCE-74, *Down Home Blues*, an album of piano solos in which "Miss Otis Regrets" and "M. H. Blues" are especially fine.

Art has also made six LPs for Delmark; my personal favorites are the quartet cuts on Delmark DS-211, *Bucket's Got a Hole in It*, and the trio cuts on Delmark DS-213, *Hodes' Art*. Both groups are notable for the interplay between musicians. Delmark (4243 N. Lincoln Avenue, Chicago, IL 60618; 312-528-8834) is one of several labels owned by Bob Koester, who is also the owner of one of the country's major jazz record stores, The Jazz Record Mart (11 W. Grand Avenue, Chicago, IL 60610; 312-222-1467).

Euphonic ESR-1213, *I Remember Bessie*, and Euphonic ESR-1218, *When Music Was Music*, are both well-chosen and well-played collections of piano solos (and, unlike Euphonic ESR-1207, well recorded). I prefer ESR-1218. Euphonic is owned and produced by Paul E. Affeldt, 357 Leighton Drive, Ventura, CA 93001. Affeldt is also the editor and publisher of *Jazz Report*, a little magazine for which Art wrote eleven articles; several of them provided materials for this book.

Sackville 3039, *Art Hodes: Blues in the Night* (Sackville Recordings, Box 87, Station J, Toronto, Ontario M4J4X8, Canada) is a stunningly good collection of piano solos. So is Parkwood 108, *Joy to the Jazz World* (Parkwood Records, Box 174, Windsor, Ontario N9A 4HO, Canada or Box 681, Detroit, MI 48231). The latter, as the title implies, is a collection of Christmas carols and songs. There is not a trace of gimmickry about it—not the slightest hint of "jazzing the classics," as the repulsive old phrase has it. As Whitney Balliett put it in his *New Yorker* profile, Art "makes rags and 'The Sunny Side of the Street' and 'The Battle Hymn of the Republic' and 'Ain't She Sweet' sound like blues." He also makes "What Child Is This" ("Greensleeves") and "Silent Night" sound like blues. But it is more than making Christmas carols into blues. These are serious, reflective, and thoroughly original sets of variations on overly familiar melodies. They are constantly surprising and a constant joy.

A recent cassette, Parkwood PW113, *Art Hodes & Marcus Belgrave: Hot 'n Cool Blues,* pairs Art with a bop trumpet player who, like the late Pee Wee Russell, takes major chances with his embouchure in the interest of achieving a remarkable variety of timbres on his horn. Like Pee Wee, he occasionally loses control, but occasional fluffs are more than justified by a sound that is moving and entertaining and unmistakably his own. His music, like Art's, is based on the blues, and the two of them achieve a tight rapport that demonstrates how very wrong it is to think that traditional jazz and bop have little in common. The success of this unorthodox pairing makes one realize how much was lost when the plans for pairing Art with Lester Young in a recording studio were cancelled by the jazz wars.

This note has necessarily been limited to pointing out a representative selection of Art's recordings, including some of my personal favorites. Many more records, cassettes, and compact discs are available at this writing, and almost certainly more will become available between this writing and publication. Also, some recordings are now out of press. Of the latter, the absence of three LPs is particularly regrettable. Mercury MG 20185, *Art Hodes and his High-Fivers: Jazz Chicago Style,* is by one version of the 1950-58 band. As Art says, "It had spirit and it had musicianship." Emarcy MGE 26005 / SRE 66005, *Art Hodes and Truck Parham: Plain Old Blues,* is an album of piano and string bass. On the advice of a studio musician, Art plays an octave higher than usual, and this gives his work less weight, but otherwise this is one of his best LPs. Muse MR 5279, *Art Hodes with Milt Hinton: Just the Two of Us,* is another piano and bass album. It may well be the best of all Art's recorded work. The interplay between the two instruments is musical conversation of a very high order. "There's an instant rapport," as Art says in the liner notes. "We speak the same language—our roots, our background. It's almost like we're from the same neighborhood. And we are, figuratively."

In 1962 Rolph Fairchild of Ontario, California, published his *Discography of Art Hodes,* a thirty-six-page booklet, covering Art's recordings from his date with Wingy Manone on December 17, 1928, through a date with Clancy Hayes for Audio Fidelity on April 11, 1960. The discography that follows is best described in the words of the compiler, Howard Rye:

The Fairchild discography is brought up to date in the present volume, but for reasons of space only original issues can be listed; these have in many cases long been withdrawn from the market.

Some of the recordings Art has made with local bands on his travels may prove difficult to obtain outside their local territories. Those on the Fat Cat's Jazz label were elusive even when in catalog, which is the reason that full discographical details have proved impossible to obtain for some of them. Since the death of the label's proprietor, Johnson "Fat Cat" McCree, most, if not all, are likely to be unavailable for the time being.

Chadwick Hansen

Discography

This discography aims to include all recordings on which Art Hodes appears and which have been issued in an edition, whether for sale or distribution to the general public or to a more limited audience (e.g. radio stations). It also aims to include known unissued performances from sessions that are included. Other performances which are known to have survived are also included up to 1950, but no attempt has been made to include such material from the era of domestic tape recording, since the number of taped performances in existence is likely to be much in excess of the space available, and it is impossible to make any prediction as to which of these may in the future be issued in some form or other.

For space reasons, only original issues are shown. Exceptionally, where the original issue was a 16″ transcription issued for sale or distribution to radio stations, the first known public issue is generally footnoted, and in cases where a later issue which contained new material includes all the performances from the original issue (e.g. a CD superseding an LP or Cassette), a note to this effect is generally made. Where a CD and LP were issued simultaneously, with additional performances on the former, the CD is treated as the original issue and the LP ignored.

Prior to 1950, all records listed in Roman type are 10″ 78 rpm discs unless noted as 12″ or as 16″ ETs (electrical transcriptions for use by radio stations); LP issues are shown in italics. After 1950, all original issues are 12″ LPs unless noted as 10″ or CDs or Cassettes and all issues are shown in Roman type. The changeover point is indicated in the text.

This project has aroused enthusiasm from everyone consulted, which is no doubt a tribute to the high musical and personal regard in which Art Hodes is held by jazz enthusiasts. Nonetheless, I must offer particular thanks to Derek Coller, Charlie Crump, and Bert Whyatt, for assistance well beyond the call of duty. My thanks also to Paul Affeldt (Euphonic Records), Dave Bennett, Dave Carey, Peter Carr, Pete Goulding, Pat Hawes, John Holley, George Hulme, Harold Jones, Bob Koester (Delmark Records), Hugh Leal (Parkwood Records), John Petters, Bill Price, Len Salmon, Alyn Shipton, Dan Simms (who generously provided information collected for his forthcoming discography of Wild Bill Davison) and, of course, Chadwick Hansen and Art Hodes. If anyone who assisted my helpers has been inadvertently omitted, I trust they will accept my apologies and my assurance that their contribution was no less appreciated for having become anonymous.

Abbreviations

AFRS	Armed Forces Radio Service	p	piano
as	alto saxophone	sb	double bass
b-t	bass trumpet	sp	speech
bar	baritone saxophone	ss	soprano saxophone
bj	banjo	t	trumpet
bsx	bass saxophone	tb	trombone
c	cornet	ts	tenor saxophone
CD	Compact Disc	tu	tuba
cl	clarinet	v	vocal
d	drums	vb	vibraphone
eb	electric bass	vn	violin
eg	electric guitar	VOA	Voice of America
ET	Electrical Transcription	vtb	valve-trombone
g	guitar	wb	washboard
h	harmonica		
OICCA	Office of International		
	Information and Cultural Affairs		

Countries of Origin

All issues listed are of United States origin, unless coded after the label name, as follows:

(As)	Austrian		(E)	British
(Au)	Australian		(G)	German
(Ca)	Canadian		(J)	Japanese
(Da)	Danish			

Bibliography

The following works have been consulted:

Walter Bruynincx, *Swing Discography, Swing//1920-1985, Swing/Dance Bands & Combos* (12 vols), Mechelen, Belgium, 1986-1990.

Walter Bruynincx, *Traditional Discography, Traditional Jazz//1897-1985 Origins/New Orleans/Dixieland/Chicago Styles* (6 vols), Mechelen, Belgium, 1987-1990.

Walter Bruynincx, *Vocalists Discography, The Vocalists 1917-1986 Singers & Crooners* (4 vols), Mechelen, Belgium, 1989-1990.

Michael Cuscuna, discography for *The Complete Blue Note Recordings Of Sidney Bechet*, Mosaic MR6-110.

Michael Cuscuna, discography for *The Complete Blue Note Recordings Of Art Hodes*, Mosaic MR5-114.

Jan Evensmo, *The Tenor Saxophone And Clarinet of Lester Young 1936–1949*, Oslo. 1983.

Rolph Fairchild, *Discography Of Art Hodes*, Ontario, Cal., 1961.

Jorgen Grunnet Jepsen, *Jazz Records, 1942-1962/1969, A Discography* (11 vols), Copenhagen or Holte, Denmark, 1963-1970.

Jack Litchfield, *This Is Jazz*, Montréal, P. Q, 1985

Hans J. Mauerer, *A Discography Of Sidney Bechet*, Copenhagen, Denmark, 1969.

Erik Raben (ed.), *Jazz Records 1942-80, A Discography*, Copenhagen, Denmark, 1989- (in progress).

Brian Rust, *Jazz Records 1897-1942*, 5th Revised and Enlarged Edition, Chigwell, Essex, n.d. [1984].

Various issues of the *Bielefelder Katalog Jazz*, and of *Collectors Items magazine*.

Joe 'Wingy' Mannone And His Club Royale Orchestra

Wingy Manone, c/v; Frank Teschemacher, cl; George Snurpus, ts; Art Hodes, p; Ray Biondi, g; Augie Schellang(e), d.

Chicago, Ill.   7 December 1928

| C-2682- | Trying To Stop My Crying | Vocalion 15797 |
| C-2683- | Isn't There A Little Love | Vocalion 15797 |

Art Hodes

Art Hodes, p solo.

New York City.   10 August 1939

R-2196	untitled original	Solo Art rejected
R-2197	Ross Tavern Boogie	Solo Art 12007
R-2198	South Side Shuffle	Solo Art 12007
R-2199	South Side Shuffle	Solo Art 12007
R-2200	untitled original	Solo Art rejected

Two different compositions were issued as *South Side Shuffle* on different editions of Solo Art 12007.

New York City.   March (or poss. January) 1940

1501-	A Selection From The Gutter	Signature 9001
1502-	Organ Grinder Blues	Signature 9001
HS-1202-	Bed Rock Blues	Jazz Record 1002
JR-101-	No Pay Blues	Jazz Record 1005
JR-102-	The Mooche	Jazz Record 1005
JR-103-	Washboard Blues	Jazz Record 1004
JR-104-	Eccentric	Jazz Record 1004
	Doin' The New Low Down	Solo Art rejected
	The Moon Of Manakoora	Solo Art rejected
	unknown title	Solo Art rejected

All the above titles were made for Solo Art at a single session; the 'matrix numbers' quoted were allocated by the issuing labels at the time of issue, and do not indicate the true order of recording.

Art Hodes' Blue Three

Rod Cless, cl; Art Hodes, p; Jimmy Butts, sb.

New York City.   c. May 1940

1600-	I've Found A New Baby	Signature 101
1600-	I've Found A New Baby (alt take)	Jazz J104
1601-	Four Or Five Times	Signature 101
1601-	Four Or Five Times (alt take)	Jazz J104
1602-	Tin Roof Blues	Signature 102
1602-	Tin Roof Blues (alt take)	Jazz J101
1603-	Diga Diga Doo	Signature 102
1603-	Diga Diga Doo (alt take)	Jazz J101

Although the Jazz and Signature issues are normally stated to use different takes, Walter Bruynincx states that he has compared one pair of titles (he does not say which) and found them to be identical.

Chicago Rhythm Kings

Marty Marsala, t; Rod Cless, cl; Art Hodes, p; Jack Goss, g; Earl Murphy, sb.

New York City.   17 August 1940

1604-	Song Of The Wanderer	Signature 104
1605-	There'll Be Some Changes Made	Signature 104
1606-	Sugar	Signature 105
1607-	Randolph Street Rag	Signature 105

Art Hodes Columbia Quintet

Duke DuVal, t; George Brunies, tb; Rod Cless, cl; Art Hodes, p; Joe Grauso, d.

New York City.   December 1940

HS-1200-	103rd Street Boogie	Jazz Record 1001
HS-1201-	Royal Garden Blues	Jazz Record 1001
HS-1204-	At The Jazz Band Ball	Jazz Record 1003
HS-1205-	Farewell Blues	Jazz Record 1003
	Sister Kate	Jazz Record rejected

The 'matrix numbers' were allocated by Jazz Record at the time of issue in 1943. For HS-1202, see January/March 1940; for HS-1203, see early 1944.

Matinee Jam Session

Shad Collins, t; J.C. Higginbotham, tb; Lester Young, ts; Joe Sullivan, Art Hodes, Sammy Price, p; Harold West, d (and possibly others including: Marty Marsala, Max Kaminsky, t; Rod Cless, cl; Lester Brown, cl/as; Coleman Hawkins, ts; Pete Johnson, p; Teddy Bunn, g).

Village Vanguard, New York City.   29 December 1940

unknown titles   unissued [ET]

This session is known to have been transcribed by Ralph Berton and possibly broadcast over Station WNYC. No further details are available.

Art Hodes and His Orchestra

Sidney DeParis, t; Brad Gowans, vtb; Rod Cless, cl; Art Hodes, p; Eddie Condon, g; Earl Murphy, sb; Zutty Singleton, d.

New York City.   17 March 1942

70519-A	Georgia Cake Walk	Decca 18437
70519-B	Georgia Cake Walk	Brunswick(E) O3438
70520-B	Liberty Inn Drag	Decca 18437
70521-A	Indiana	Decca 18438
70521-B	Indiana	Decca 18438
70522-A	Get Happy	Decca 18438

Art Hodes

Art Hodes, p solo.

New York City   17 July 1942

54-RS	Snowy Morning Blues	Black & White 1
55-RS	Four Or Five Times	Black & White 1
2A-(3)	Art's Boogie	Black & White 2
2B-(4)	St. Louis Blues	Black & White 2
	Sad And Blue	Black & White unissued
	Dear Old Southland	Black & White unissued
	She Went And Did Her Dance	Black & White unissued

These titles were originally recorded for the private collection of Les Schreiber, the future proprietor of Black & White; the 'matrix numbers' were allocated at the time of issue.

New York City.   July 1942
              Eccentric   Black & White unissued
              How Long Blues   Black & White unissued
These titles were originally recorded for the private collection of Les Schreiber, the future proprietor of Black & White.

New York City.   late 1943 or early 1944
HS-1203-   You've Got To Give Me Some   Jazz Record 1002
According to the review in *Jazz Record No.20* (May 1944), this title had been newly recorded to provide a backing for the Solo Art version of *Bed Rock Blues*, but no more specific information is available.

Art Hodes' Trio
Milton 'Mezz' Mezzrow, cl; Art Hodes, p; Danny Alvin, d.
  New York City.   5 March 1944
F-162   Feather's Lament   Session 10-007
F-163   Messin' Around   Session 10-007

Mezz Mezzrow Trio
Milton 'Mezz' Mezzrow, cl; Art Hodes, p; Danny Alvin, d.
  New York City.   15 March 1944
F-160   Really The Blues   Session 10-008
F-161   Milk For Mezz   Session 10-008

Art Hodes' Chicagoans
Max Kaminsky, t; Ray Conniff, tb; Rod Cless, cl; Art Hodes, p; Jack Bland, g; Bob Haggart, sb; Danny Alvin, d.
  New York City.   18 March 1944
BN-960-0   Maple Leaf Rag   Blue Note 505
BN-960-1   Maple Leaf Rag   *Blue Note B6508*
BN-961-1   She's Crying For Me   Blue Note 506
BN-962-0   Yellow Dog Blues   Blue Note 505
BN-963-1   Slow 'Em Down Blues   *Blue Note B6508*
BN-963-2   Slow 'Em Down Blues   Blue Note 506

Max Kaminsky, t; Ray Conniff, tb; Rod Cless, cl; Art Hodes, p; Jack Bland, g; Sid Jacobs, sb; Danny Alvin, d.
  New York City.   22 March 1944
BN-964-2   Doctor Jazz   Blue Note 507
BN-965-2   Shoe Shiner's Drag   Blue Note 507
BN-966-1   There'll Be Some Changes Made   *Mosaic MR5-114*
BN-966-4   There'll Be Some Changes Made   Blue Note 508
BN-967-0   Clark And Randolph   Blue Note 508
Blue Note B6508 claims to use BN-964-1. The producers of Mosaic MR5-114 state that this claim is incorrect but other sources have reported that it is in fact an aurally distinct version.

Art Hodes' Back Room Boys
Max Kaminsky, t-1; Sandy Williams, tb-2; Art Hodes, p; James Arthur 'Jimmy' Shirley, g; Israel Crosby, sb.

New York City.   21 April 1944

BN-968-0	M.K. Blues -1	Blue Note 527
BN-968-1	M.K. Blues -1	*Blue Note B6508*
BN-969-0	Low Down Blues -2	Blue Note 526
BN-970-0	Jug Head Boogie -1, 2	*Blue Note B6508*
BN-970-1	Jug Head Boogie -1, 2	Blue Note 527
BN-970-2	Jug Head Boogie -1, 2	*Mosaic MR5-114*
BN-971-0	S.C.H. Blues	*Mosaic MR5-114*
BN-972-0	Back Room Blues	Blue Note 526

Some reissues of BN-969 show the title as *Low Down Bama Blues.*

Art Hodes' Blue Note Jazzmen
Max Kaminsky, t; Vic Dickenson, tb; Edmond Hall, cl; Art Hodes, p; Jimmy Shirley, g; Sid Weiss, sb; Danny Alvin, d.

New York City   1 June 1944

BN-977-0	Sweet Georgia Brown	Blue Note 34 [12"]
BN-978-0	Squeeze Me	Blue Note 35 [12"]
BN-978-1	Squeeze Me	*Blue Note B6504*
BN-979-0	Sugar Foot Stomp	*Blue Note B6504*
BN-979-1	Sugar Foot Stomp	Blue Note 34 [12"]
BN-980-0	Bugle Call Rag	*Blue Note B6504*
BN-980-1	Bugle Call Rag	Blue Note 35 [12"]
BN-980-2	Bugle Call Rag No.2	*Blue Note B6504*

Art Hodes
Art Hodes, p solo.

Town Hall, New York City.   26 August 1944

Beale Street Blues   AFRS Eddie Condon #13 [16" ET]

This title was transcribed from Eddie Condon Blue Network Show #15, and has been commercially issued on *Jazum 25.*

Art Hodes' Blue Five
Max Kaminsky, t; Milton 'Mezz' Mezzrow, cl; Art Hodes, p; George 'Pops' Foster, sb; Danny Alvin, d.

New York City.   11 December 1944

BN-200-0	Gutbucket Blues	Blue Note 528
BN-201-1	Apex Blues	Blue Note 45 [12"]
BN-202-0	Shake That Thing	*Blue Note B6502*
BN-202-1	Shake That Thing	Blue Note 45 [12"]
BN-203-0	Indiana	*Blue Note(J) K23P-9288*
BN-204-0	Nobody's Sweetheart	Blue Note 528
BN-204-1	Nobody's Sweetheart	*Blue Note(J) K23P-9288*

Blue Note B6502 claims incorrectly to use BN-202-1; this applies to some other LPs also.

Art Hodes Trio
Milton 'Mezz' Mezzrow, cl; Art Hodes, p; Danny Alvin, d/v-1.

New York City.   12 December 1944

N-2934-1	Apex Blues	*Jazzology J104*
N-2934-2	Apex Blues (incomplete)	*Jazzology J104*
N-2934-3	Apex Blues	World Feature Jam Sessions JS42 [ET]
N-2935-1	Sweet Sue (incomplete)	*Jazzology J104*
N-2935-2	Sweet Sue	World Feature Jam Sessions JS41 [ET]
N-2936-1	52nd Street Getaway	*Jazzology J104*
N-2936-2	52nd Street Getaway	World Feature Jam Sessions JS42 [ET]
N-2936-3	52nd Street Getaway (false start)	*Jazzology J104*
N-2936-4	52nd Street Getaway	*Jazzology J104*
N-2937-1	The Professor In Mind	World Feature Jam Sessions JS41 [ET]
N-2938-1	Ugly Child -1 (false start)	*Jazzology J104*
N-2938-2	Ugly Child -1	*Jazzology J104*
N-2938-3	Ugly Child -1	*Jazzology J104*
N-2938-4	Ugly Child -1 (false start)	*Jazzology J104*
N-2938-5	Ugly Child -1 (incomplete)	*Jazzology J104*
N-2938-6	Ugly Child -1	*Jazzology J104*
N-2938-7	Ugly Child -1 (incomplete)	*Jazzology J104*
N-2938-8	Ugly Child -1	World Feature Jam Sessions JS41 [ET]
N-2939-1	I Wish I Could Shimmy Like My Sister Kate -1	*Jazzology J104*
N-2939-2	I Wish I Could Shimmy Like My Sister Kate -1	World Feature Jam Sessions JS41 [ET]
N-2940-1	Bugle Call Rag (incomplete)	*Jazzology J104*
N-2940-2	Bugle Call Rag	*Jazzology J104*
N-2940-3	Bugle Call Rag (false start)	*Jazzology J104*
N-2940-4	Bugle Call Rag	World Feature Jam Sessions JS42 [ET]
N-2941-1	The Sheik Of Araby	*Jazzology J104*
N-2941-2	The Sheik Of Araby	World Feature Jam Sessions JS42 [ET]
N-2942-1	Really The Blues	World Feature Jam Sessions JS42 [ET]
N-2943-1	My Daddy Rocks Me (incomplete)	*Jazzology J104*
N-2943-2	My Daddy Rocks Me	World Feature Jam Sessions JS41 [ET]

All titles from this session have been issued commercially on *Jazzology J104*.

Sidney Bechet Blue Note Jazzmen

Sidney DeParis, t; Vic Dickenson, tb; Sidney Bechet, cl-1/ss-2; Art Hodes, p; George 'Pops' Foster, sb; Manzie Johnson, d.

New York City.   20 December 1944

BN-206-1	St. Louis Blues -1	Blue Note 44 [12"]
BN-207-0	Jazz Me Blues -1	*Mosaic MR6-110*
BN-207-3	Jazz Me Blues -1	Blue Note 44 [12"]
BN-208-0	Blue Horizon -1	Blue Note 43 [12"]
BN-209-0	Muskrat Ramble -2	Blue Note 43 [12"]

Max Kaminsky, t; George Lugg, tb; Sidney Bechet, cl-1/ss-2; Art Hodes, p; George 'Pops' Foster, sb; Fred Moore, d/v-3.

New York City.   21 January 1945

BN-215-1	High Society -1	Blue Note 50 [12"]
BN-216-2	Salty Dog -1, 3	Blue Note 49 [12"]
BN-217-1	Weary Blues -2	Blue Note 49 [12"]
BN-218-1	Jackass Blues -2	*Mosaic MR6-110*
BN-218-2	Jackass Blues -2	Blue Note 50 [12"]

The date quoted for this session is as given by Mosaic; other sources have given 27 or 29 January 1945.

Original Art Hodes Trio

Max Kaminsky, t; Art Hodes, p; Fred Moore, d/v-1.

New York City.   6 April 1945

BN-229-3	That Eccentric Rag	*Blue Note B6508*
BN-229-4	Eccentric	Blue Note 512
BN-230-0	K.M.H. Drag	Blue Note 51 [12"]
BN-231-1	Funny Feathers	Blue Note 51 [12"]
BN-232-0	Blues 'N' Booze -1	Blue Note 512

K.M.H. Drag has been reissued as *Draggin' The Blues*.

Art Hodes' Hot Seven

Max Kaminsky, t; George Lugg, tb-1; Leonard 'Bujie' Centobie, cl; Art Hodes, p; Chick Robertson, g; Jack Lesberg, sb; Danny Alvin, d.

New York City.   17 May 1945

BN-237-1	Chicago Gal -1	Blue Note 552
BN-238-3	I Never Knew What A Gal Could Do -1	Blue Note 551
BN-239-1	Mr. Jelly Lord -1	Blue Note 551
BN-240-3	At The Jazz Band Ball -1	*Mosaic MR5-114*

New York City.   22 May 1945

BN-241-0	Wolverine Blues -1	Blue Note 550
BN-242-4	Milenberg Joys -1	*Blue Note BLP7015*
BN-243-0	Walk On Down -1	*Blue Note BLP7015*
BN-244-2	Willie The Weeper -1	Blue Note 552
BN-244-3	Willie The Weeper -1	*Blue Note B6509*
BN-245-0	Bujie Blues	Blue Note 550

Art Hodes' Back Room Boys

Oliver 'Rev' Mesheux, t; Omer Simeon, cl; Art Hodes, p.; Al Lucas, sb; Fred Moore, d.

New York City.   14 September 1945

BN-258-2	None Of My Jelly Roll (#1)	*Mosaic MR5-114*
BN-258-4	None Of My Jelly Roll (#2)	*Mosaic MR5-114*
BN-259-0	Blues For Jelly (alt #1)	*Blue Note B6509*
BN-259-1	Blues For Jelly (alt #2)	*Blue Note B6502*
BN-259-2	Blues For Jelly	*Blue Note BLP7021*
BN-261-0	Jack Daily Blues	*Blue Note BLP7021*
BN-260-2	Beale Street Blues	*Mosaic MR5-114*

Art Hodes' Hot Five

Wild Bill Davison, c; Sidney Bechet, cl-1/ss-2; Art Hodes, p; George 'Pops' Foster, sb; Fred Moore, d/v-3.

New York City		12 October 1945
BN-262-1	Save It Pretty Mama -1	Blue Note 531
BN-263-1	Way Down Yonder In New Orleans -1	Blue Note 533
BN-264-1	Memphis Blues -2	Blue Note 532
BN-265-0	Shine -2	Blue Note 532
BN-266-1	St. James Infirmary -2, 3	Blue Note 533
BN-267-0	Darktown Strutters' Ball -2	Blue Note 531
BN-267-2	Darktown Strutters' Ball -1	*Mosaic MR6-110*

Baby Dodds Jazz Four

Albert Nicholas, cl; Art Hodes, p; Wellman Braud, sb; Warren 'Baby' Dodds, d.

New York City.		16 December 1945
BN-272-2	Feelin' At Ease	Blue Note 519
BN-273-2	Careless Love	Blue Note 518
BN-273-4	Careless Love	*Mosaic MR5-114*
BN-273-5	Careless Love	*Blue Note BLP7021*
BN-274-0	High Society	*Mosaic MR5-114*
BN-274-2	High Society	Blue Note 519
BN-275-0	Winin' Boy Blues	Blue Note 518

Creole Gayno [*sic*]

Henry Goodwin, t; Art Hodes, p; Jimmy Shirley, g; George 'Pops' Foster, sb; 'Creole' George Guesnon, v.

New York City.		1946
LR-122	Graveyard Love Blues	Lissen 1043
LR-124	Top And Bottom Blues	Lissen 1043

Matrix LR-123 is untraced.

Bechet-Nicholas Blue Five

Albert Nicholas, cl; Sidney Bechet, cl-1/ss-2; Art Hodes, p; George 'Pops' Foster, sb; Danny Alvin, d.

New York City.		12 February 1946
BN-276-0	Blame It On The Blues -2	*Mosaic MR6-110*
BN-276-1	Quincy Street Stomp -2	Blue Note 517
BN-277-1	Old Stack O'Lee Blues -1	Blue Note 54 [12"]
BN-278-3	Bechet's Fantasy -2	Blue Note 54 [12"]
BN-279-0	Weary Way Blues -1	*Blue Note BLP7008*
BN-279-2	Weary Way Blues -1	Blue Note 517

Reissues of *Quincy Street Stomp* are titled *Blame It On The Blues.*

Art Hodes' Jazz Record Six

Henry Goodwin, t; George Lugg, tb; Cecil Scott, cl; Art Hodes, p; George 'Pops' Foster, sb; Kaiser Marshall, d.

New York City.		15 March 1946
301	Chimes Blues	Jazz Record 1006
302-B	Sister Kate	Jazz Record rejected
303	Wolverine Blues	Jazz Record 1007
304-B	Someday Sweetheart	Jazz Record 1007
305-B	Basin Street Blues	Jazz Record rejected
306-C	That's A Plenty	Jazz Record rejected
307	Organ Grinder Blues	Jazz Record 1006
	Muskrat Ramble	Jazz Record rejected

New York City.   20 March 1946
302-A   Sister Kate   Jazz Record 1008
304-A   Someday Sweetheart   Jazz Record unissued
305   Basin Street Blues   Jazz Record 1008
306   That's A Plenty   Jazz Record 1009
308   Ballin' The Jack   Jazz Record 1009
             Tin Roof Blues   Jazz Record unissued
             Clarinet Marmalade   Jazz Record unissued
             Muskrat Ramble   Jazz Record unissued

Henry Goodwin, t; Cecil Scott, cl; Sonny Terry, h/v; Art Hodes, p; Cow Cow Davenport, p/v; Brownie McGhee, g/v; George 'Pops' Foster, sb; Kaiser Marshall, d.

New York City.   c. 21 March 1946
309   Cake Walking Babies   Jazz Record unissued
310   Backwater Blues   Jazz Record unissued
311   Sonny Terry's Low Down Blues Jazz Record unissued
312   Brownie's Blues   Jazz Record unissued

No information is available about the allocation of vocals on these unissued sides beyond what can be deduced from the titles. Rights in these recordings were transferred to Atlantic Records; Rolph Fairchild reported that Atlantic were unable to locate them and doubted that they were still extant.

Art Hodes' Band

Henry Goodwin, t; George Lugg, tb; Cecil Scott, cl; Art Hodes, p; George 'Pops' Foster, sb; Warren 'Baby' Dodds, d.

New York City.   29 June 1946
             Basin Street Blues — Pt. I   unissued
             Basin Street Blues — Pt. II   unissued
             Squeeze Me   unissued
             Royal Garden Blues   unissued

These acetates are from a WNYC *Jazz Classics* broadcast.

Jazz At The Town Hall

Muggsy Spanier, t; Irving 'Miff' Mole, tb; Pee Wee Russell, cl; Art Hodes, p; George 'Pops' Foster, sb; George Wettling, d.

Town Hall, New York City.   21 September 1946
             Royal Garden Blues   *Xtra(E) XTRA1003*
             How Come You Do Me Like You Do *Xtra(E) XTRA1003*
             Relaxing At The Touro   *Folkways FJ2841*

Wild Bill Davison, c; Johnny Windhurst, t; Irving 'Miff' Mole, tb; Pee Wee Russell, Milton 'Mezz' Mezzrow, cl; Art Hodes, James P. Johnson, p; George 'Pops' Foster, sb; Warren 'Baby' Dodds, d.

Same concert.
             The Blues   *Xtra(E) XTRA1043*

Wild Bill Davison, c; Johnny Windhurst, t; Vernon Brown, tb; Milton 'Mezz' Mezzrow, cl; Art Hodes, p; George 'Pops' Foster, sb; George Wettling, d.

Same concert.
             Jazz Me Blues   *Xtra(E) XTRA1003*

All titles from this concert were first issued on *Folkways FJ2841*, but most, if not all, are severely edited.

Pops Foster's Ragtimers
Henry Goodwin, t; George Lugg, tb; Cecil Scott, cl; Art Hodes, p; Eddie Gibbs, bj;
George 'Pops' Foster, sb; Danny Alvin, d.
   New York City.   25 October 1946
           Clarinet Marmalade   Jazz Record unissued

Baby Dodds' Band
Wild Bill Davison, c; George Lugg, tb; Tony Parenti, cl; Art Hodes, p; Eddie Gibbs, bj;
George 'Pops' Foster, sb; Warren 'Baby' Dodds, d.
   New York City.   25 October 1946
           Ballin' The Jack   Jazz Record unissued
           Fidgety Feet   Jazz Record unissued

Jazz At The Town Hall
Sidney DeParis, t; Wilbur DeParis, tb; Sidney Bechet, cl/ss; Art Hodes, p; George 'Pops'
Foster, sb; Warren 'Baby' Dodds, d.
   Town Hall, New York City.   26 October 1946
           Dippermouth Blues   unissued
Sidney DeParis, t; Albert Nicholas, cl; Art Hodes, p; George 'Pops' Foster, sb; Warren
'Baby' Dodds, d.
   Same concert.
           Clarinet Marmalade   unissued
Wilbur DeParis, tb; Tony Parenti, cl; Art Hodes, p; George 'Pops' Foster, sb; Warren
'Baby' Dodds, d.
   Same concert.
           Grace And Beauty   unissued

The Really The Blues Concert
Muggsy Spanier, c; Sandy Williams, tb; Milton 'Mezz' Mezzrow, cl; Sidney Bechet, ss;
Art Hodes, p; Wellman Braud, sb; Warren 'Baby' Dodds, d.
   Town Hall, New York City.   9 November 1946
           There'll Be Some Changes Made   *Jazz Archives JA39*
           Friar's Point Shuffle   *Jazz Archives JA39*
           Really The Blues   *Jazz Archives JA39*
           Really The Blues (Extension)   *Jazz Archives JA39*
Johnny Glasel, t; Bob Mielke, tb; Bob Wilber, ss; Dick Wellstood, p; Charlie Traeger,
sb; Denny Strong, d, added.
   Same concert.
           High Society   *Jazz Archives JA39*
The sleeve of *Jazz Archives JA39* incorrectly dates this concert to 1 January 1947 and
gives the pianist as Sammy Price, who appears on other titles from the concert.

All Star Stompers
Muggsy Spanier, c; Georg Brunis, tb/v-1; Albert Nicholas, cl; Sidney Bechet, ss; Art
Hodes, p; Danny Barker, g; George 'Pops' Foster, sb; Warren 'Baby' Dodds, d/v.
   New York City.   24 March 1947
(1)   Sensation Rag   OICCA Notes On Jazz # 20 [16" ET]
(2)   You're Some Pretty Doll (Ugly Chile) -1 *Rarities(E) 35*
(5)   Black And Blue   VOA American Jazz #56 [16" ET]
(6)   Summertime   VOA American Jazz #56 [16" ET]
(7)   Farewell Blues   *Rarities(E) 35*
Albert Nicholas, cl; Art Hodes, p; Danny Barker, g; George 'Pops' Foster, sb; Warren

'Baby' Dodds, d/v.
  Same session.
(4)   Buddy Bolden's Blues   OICCA Notes On Jazz # 20 [16" ET]
Art Hodes, p solo.
  Same session.
(3)   Twelfth Street Rag   VOA American Jazz #56 [16" ET]
These titles comprise a Mutual Broadcasting System *This Is Jazz* broadcast, and have
been listed out of order for clarity; the bracketed numerals in the matrix-number
column indicate the actual order of the broadcast. The issues cited are believed to be
the earliest; the whole session has been issued on *Rarities(E) 35* and *Rhapsody(E)
RHA6037.*

All Star Trio
Art Hodes, p/v-1; George 'Pops' Foster, sb; Warren 'Baby' Dodds, d/v-2.
  New York City.   27 March 1947
314   Buddy Bolden's Blues   Jazz Record 1010
315   Droppin' Shucks -1   Jazz Record 1011
316   Black And Blue -1   Jazz Record unissued
317   untitled original rag by Art Hodes   Jazz Record unissued
318   Too Busy -2   Jazz Record 1010
319   Swanee   Jazz Record 1011
                 Panama   Jazz Record unissued
Rolph Fairchild states that *Panama* was issued on 'AFRS' (OICCA) Notes On Jazz #20
[16" ET], but other sources show this as by the All Star Stompers, without Art Hodes,
from the broadcast of 8 March 1947.

All Star Stompers
Muggsy Spanier, c; Georg Brunis, tb; Albert Nicholas, cl; Art Hodes, p; Danny Barker,
g; George 'Pops' Foster, sb.
  New York City.   12 April 1947
(1)   There'll Be Some Changes Made   unissued
(2)   Heartaches   unissued
(3)   My Honey's Lovin' Arms   unissued
(6)   Ja Da   unissued
(8)   When The Saints Go Marching In   unissued
Art Hodes, p; Danny Barker, g; George 'Pops' Foster, sb.
  Same session
(7)   Organ Grinder Blues   unissued
These titles are from a Mutual Broadcasting System *This Is Jazz* broadcast, and have
been listed out of order for clarity; the bracketed numerals in the matrix-number
column indicate the actual order of the broadcast. Art Hodes did not take part in the
omitted performances.

Wild Bill Davison, c; Louis Armstrong, t/v-1; Georg Brunis, tb; Albert Nicholas, cl; Art
Hodes, p; Danny Barker, g; George 'Pops' Foster, sb; Warren 'Baby' Dodds, d.
  New York City.   26 April 1947
       When The Saints Go Marching In -1   OICCA Notes On Jazz # 23 [16" ET]
       2:19 Blues -1   OICCA Notes On Jazz # 23 [16" ET]
       Do You Know What It Means To Miss
       New Orleans -1   VOA American Jazz #53 [16" ET]
       Dipper Mouth Blues   *Fairmont F108*
       Basin Street Blues -1   OICCA Notes On Jazz # 23 [16" ET]
       High Society   OICCA Notes On Jazz # 23 [16" ET]

I'll Be Glad When You're Dead,
You Rascal You -1   *Fairmont F108*
These titles comprise a Mutual Broadcasting System *This Is Jazz* broadcast. The
issues cited are believed to be the earliest; the whole session has been issued under
Louis Armstrong's name on *Fairmont F108* and *Music For Pleasure(F) 2M146-13271.*

Wild Bill Davison, Johnny Glasel -1, c; Georg Brunis, tb; Albert Nicholas, cl; Art
Hodes, p; Danny Barker, g; George 'Pops' Foster, sb; Warren 'Baby' Dodds, d.
New York City.   17 May 1947
           Original Dixieland One-Step   unissued
           I Ain't Got Nobody   unissued
           Hotter Than That   unissued
           Shine -1   unissued
           Memphis Blues   unissued
           Yesterdays   unissued
           King Porter Stomp   unissued
These titles comprise a Mutual Broadcasting System *This Is Jazz* broadcast.

Wingy Mannone-Sidney Bechet
Wingy Manone, t/v-1; Vernon Brown, tb; Sidney Bechet, ss; Bud Freeman, ts-2; Art
Hodes, p; George 'Pops' Foster, sb; George Wettling, d.
Town Hall, New York City.   11 October 1947
           St. Louis Blues -1, 2   *Jazz Archives JA29*
           At The Jazz Band Ball   *Jazz Archives JA29*
Jimmy Archey, tb; Edmond Hall, cl; Michael 'Peanuts' Hucko, ts, probably added.
Same session.
           All-Out Jam Session
           (Bugle Call Rag) -2   unissued
Wingy Manone, t/v; Jimmy Archey, tb; Edmond Hall, cl; Michael 'Peanuts' Hucko, ts;
Art Hodes, p; George 'Pops' Foster, sb; George Wettling, d.
Same session.
           Ochi Corniya   *Jazz Archives JA29*
           On The Sunny Side Of The Street *Jazz Archives JA29*
           Early Morning Blues   *Jazz Archives JA29*
           Isle Of Capri   *Jazz Archives JA29*

Sidney Bechet's Blue Note Jazzmen
Wild Bill Davison, c; Sidney Bechet, ss; Art Hodes, p; George 'Pops' Foster, sb; Fred
Moore, d.
New York City.   21 January 1949
BN-348-2   Sister Kate   Blue Note 573
BN-349-2   Tiger Rag   Blue Note 562
BN-350-0   Tin Roof Blues   Blue Note 561
BN-351-0   I Found A New Baby   *Blue Note BLP7014*
BN-352-1   Nobody Knows You When
          You're Down And Out   Blue Note 571
BN-353-1   When The Saints Go Marchin' In   Blue Note 563

WNYC Jazz Festival
Tony Parenti, cl; Art Hodes, p.
New York City.   19 February 1949
           Twelfth Street Rag   VOA American Jazz Series #41 [ET]

| | Blues | VOA American Jazz Series #41 [ET] |
| | Eccentric Rag | VOA American Jazz Series #41 [ET] |

Gus Aiken, t; Tony Parenti, cl; Art Hodes, p; Wellman Braud, sb; prob. Fred Moore, d; Ann Lewis, v.
Same concert.

| | Fish Out Of The Water | *Jazz Unlimited JU3* |
| | Jailhouse Blues | *Jazz Unlimited JU3* |

12th Street Rag was also issued commercially on *Jazz Unlimited JU3*.

Sidney Bechet's Blue Note Jazzmen

Wild Bill Davison, c; Ray Diehl, tb; Sidney Bechet, ss; Art Hodes, p; Walter Page, sb; Wilmore 'Slick' Jones, d.
New York City.   23 March 1949

BN-354-0	Basin Street Blues	Blue Note 563
BN-355-1	Cake Walking Babies	Blue Note 562
BN-356-1	Tailgate Ramble	*Blue Note BLP7014*
BN-357-2	At The Jazz Band Ball	Blue Note 561
BN-358-0	Joshua Fit The Battle Of Jericho	*Blue Note BLP7014*
BN-359-0	Fidgety Feet	Blue Note 571

Tony Parenti And His New Orleanians

Wild Bill Davison, t/v-1; Jimmy Archey, tb/v-1; Tony Parenti, cl/v-1; Art Hodes, p; George 'Pops' Foster, sb; Arthur Trappier, d; band v-1
New York City.   16 August 1949

JA-1-1	There'll Be Some Changes Made	*Jazzology JCE1 [10"]*
JA-1-2	There'll Be Some Changes Made	Jazzology JZL3
JA-2-1	Dippermouth Blues (incomplete)	*Jazzology JCE1 [10"]*
JA-2-2	Dippermouth Blues	*Jazzology JCE1 [10"]*
JA-2-3	Dippermouth Blues	Jazzology JZL4
JA-3-1	Sunday	*Jazzology JCE1 [10"]*
JA-3-2	Sunday	Jazzology JZL3
JA-4-1	Chinatown, My Chinatown	*Jazzology JCE1 [10"]*
JA-4-2	Chinatown, My Chinatown	Jazzology JZL4

New York City.   17 August 1949

JA-5-1	When The Saints Go Marching In -1	Jazzology JZL1
JA-6-1	Blues For Faz	Jazzology JZL2
JA-7-2	Bugle Call Rag (incomplete)	*Jazzology JCE1 [10"]*
JA-7-3	Bugle Call Rag	*Jazzology JCE1 [10"]*
JA-7-4	Bugle Call Rag	*Jazzology JCE1 [10"]*
JA-7-5	Bugle Call Rag	Jazzology JZL2
JA-8-1	Moonlight On The Ganges	Jazzology JZL1
	I Found A New Baby	Jazzology unissued
	Oh Didn't He Ramble	Jazzology unissued

Art Hodes

Unknown, t; unknown, tb; unknown, cl; Art Hodes, p; unknown, sb; unknown, d.
Unknown location.   c. mid to late 1940s

	Beale Street Blues	VOA AO56 [ET]
	unknown blues	VOA AO56 [ET]
	Ballin' The Jack	VOA AO56 [ET]

Pee Wee Russell Quartet
Pee Wee Russell, cl; Art Hodes, p; unknown, sb; unknown, d.
Voice of America broadcast, unknown location.   c. 1950s

	Four Or Five Times	VOA #38 [ET];
		Shoestring SS109

No more detailed information is available about the origin of this recording.

From this point onwards, all original issues are LPs and these are no longer shown in italics.
From this point also, unissued recordings are noted only if made for or held by record companies.

Art Hodes Trio
George Lewis, cl; Art Hodes, p; Lawrence Marrero, bj.
1637 North Ashland, Chicago, Ill.   5 March 1953

Loveless Love	Paramount unissued; Jazzology J113
Sheik Of Araby	Paramount unissued; Jazzology J113
Lingering Blues	Paramount unissued; Jazzology J113

Darnell Howard, cl; Art Hodes, p; Phil Atwood, eb; Warren 'Baby' Dodds, d.
Phil Atwood's house, Chicago, Ill.   22 November 1953

112253-1a	Slow And Easy Mama	Paramount CJS112
112253-2c	I Know That You Know	Paramount CJS112
112253-3a	Baby Food	Paramount CJS112
112253-4a	Sweet Georgia Brown	Paramount CJS112

Phil Atwood was present 'off-mike' and is largely inaudible.

Voltaire 'Volly' DeFaut, cl; Art Hodes, p/sp-3; Phil Atwood, eb; Jasper Taylor, d-1/wb-2/sp-3.
Phil Atwood's house, Chicago, Ill.   10 December 1953

121053-1a	Someday Sweetheart -1	Paramount CJS112
121053-2a	Washboard Stomp -2	Paramount CJS112
121053-3b/c	Tishomingo -1, 3	Paramount CJS112
121053-4b	Copenhagen -1	Paramount CJS112

Art Hodes And His Hi-Fivers
Byrne 'Muggsy' Dawson, c; Floyd O'Brien, tb; Jimmy Granato, cl; Art Hodes, p; Earl Murphy, sb/v-1; Hap Gormley, d; band v-1
Chicago, Ill.   19 April 1954

10626	Mr. Piano Man	EmArcy MG26014 [10"]
10627	Stuff And Nonsense	EmArcy MG26014 [10"]
10628	Grandpa's Spells	EmArcy MG26014 [10"]
10629	When Jimmy Yancey Was A Young Man	EmArcy MG26014 [10"]
10630	Sweet Georgia Brown	EmArcy MG26014 [10"]
10631	Wait For Me	EmArcy MG26014 [10"]
10632	Four Or Five Times -1	EmArcy MG26014 [10"]
10633	Blues Keep Callin'	EmArcy MG26014 [10"]

Art Hodes
Art Hodes, p solo.
Chicago, Ill.   1955 (or poss. 1953)

Selection From The Basin (For Today)   unissued
Sweet Lorraine   unissued
Original Rag   unissued
Just Blues   unissued
Grandpa's Spells   unissued
Sweet Georgia Brown   unissued
Begin The Beguine   unissued
Birth Of The Blues   unissued
Ballin' The Jack   unissued
Boogie Blues (When Jimmy Yancey
Was A Young Man)   unissued

This session is a tape entitled *Rediscovered Art Hodes Piano Solos* held by John Steiner (Paramount), but never issued commercially.

Art Hodes And His Hi-Fivers

Byrne 'Muggsy' Dawson, c; Al Jenkins, tb; Jimmy Granato, cl; Art Hodes, p; John Frigo, sb; Hap Gormley, d.

Chicago, Ill.   31 July 1956

13844	Royal Garden Blues	EmArcy MG20185
13845	Organ Grinder	EmArcy MG20185
13846	Randolph And Dearborn	EmArcy MG20185
13847	South	EmArcy MG20185

Art Hodes Orchestra -1/Art Hodes Trio -2/Art Hodes-3

Fred Greenleaf, t-4; Dave Remington, tb-4; Bill Reinhardt, cl-4; Art Hodes, p; Charles 'Truck' Parham, sb-5; Fred Moore, d-6/wb-7/v-8.

Chicago, Ill.   12 June 1957

DE-100	St. Louis Blues -1, 4, 5, 6	Dotted Eighth DELP1000
DE-101	Riverside Blues -1, 4, 5, 6	Dotted Eighth DELP1000
DE-102	Livery Stable Blues -1, 4, 5, 6	Dotted Eighth DELP1000
DE-103-2	Train Leaving On Track # 10 -2, 5, 6	Dotted Eighth DELP1000
DE-104	The Mooch [sic]-3	Dotted Eighth DELP1000
DE-105-3	Blues 'N Booze -2, 5, 6	Dotted Eighth DELP1000
DE-106	Tiger Rag -2, 5, 7	Dotted Eighth DELP1000
DE-107	Washboard Blues -3	Dotted Eighth DELP1000
DE-108	I Ain't Gonna Give No One None Of My Jellyroll [sic]-2, 5, 6, 8	Dotted Eighth DELP1000
DE-109	Someone To Watch Over Me -3	Dotted Eighth DELP1000
DE-111	Portrait In Blue -3	Dotted Eighth DELP1000
	Maryland, My Maryland -3	Dotted Eighth unissued
	Jazz Unlimited -3	Dotted Eighth unissued
	Washington And Lee Swing -1, 4, 5, 6	Dotted Eighth unissued
	South Rampart Street Parade -1, 4, 5, 6	Dotted Eighth unissued
	Bourbon Street Parade -1, 4, 5, 6	Dotted Eighth unissued

Matrix DE-110 is untraced, but may be one of the unissued titles whose matrix number is unknown. However, no matrix number was allocated to the last three titles listed.

Summit Meeting

Johnny Wiggs, c-1; Raymond Burke, cl; Art Hodes, p; Edmond Souchon, g/v-2; Fred Moore, d/wb-3/v-4.

Saukville, Wis.   29 July 1957
take -c   City Of A Million Dreams -1   Jazzology J7
take -c   Postman's Lament -1, 2   Jazzology J7
             Careless Love -1   Jazzology J7
take -b   Ugly Chile -1, 4   Jazzology J7
take -b   Bye-Bye Blues -1, 3   Jazzology J7
             Eccentric   Jazzology J7
take -b   Just A Closer Walk With Thee -1 Jazzology J7

Johnny Wiggs, c; Raymond Burke, cl/h; Art Hodes, p; Edmond Souchon, g/v; Fred
Moore, d.
   Same session.
             Brown Skin Woman   Jazzology J7

Art Hodes' Quintet
Eddie Burleton, cl; Art Hodes, p; Marty Grosz, g; Charles 'Truck' Parham, sb; Freddie
Kohlman, d.
   Chicago, Ill.   8 December 1957
             Dardanella   Audiophile AP54
             After You've Gone   Audiophile AP54
             B-Flat Blues   Audiophile AP54
             Apex Blues   Audiophile AP54
             Chimes Blues   Audiophile AP54
             Ain't She Sweet   Audiophile AP54
             Angry   Audiophile AP54
             Liberty Inn Drag   Audiophile AP54
             I've Found A New Baby   Audiophile AP54

Art Hodes Orchestra/Jimmy McPartland Orchestra
Art Hodes Orchestra: Nap Trottier, t; George Brunies, tb/nose-1; Pee Wee Russell, cl;
Art Hodes, p; Earl Murphy, sb/bj-3; Buddy Smith, d.
Jimmy McPartland Orchestra: Jimmy McPartland, t/v-2; Vic Dickenson, tb; Jack
Maheu, cl; Lawrence 'Bud' Freeman, ts; Floyd Bean, p; John Frigo, sb/vn-3; George
Wettling, d.
   Chicago, Ill.   7 May 1959
18566-1   Chicago   Mercury MG20460
18567-6   Logan Square -2   Mercury MG20460
18568-1   Bill Bailey Won't You Please
             Come Home -1, 3   Mercury MG20460
18569-3   You've Gotta See Mama
             Ev'ry Night (Or You Can't
             See Mama At All)   Mercury MG20460
18570-4   Somebody Stole My Gal   Mercury MG20460
18571-2   I Never Knew (I Could Love
             Anybody, Like I'm Loving You)   Mercury MG20460
18572-3   'Deed I Do   Mercury MG20460
18573-4   I Wish I Could Shimmy
             Like My Sister Kate   Mercury MG20460
18574-3   Meet Me In Chicago   Mercury MG20460
18575-3   Runnin' Wild   Mercury unissued
Both bands are heard on each title, with soloists being backed by the rhythm section of
their own band. The term 'nose' above refers to Brunies making a sound through one
nostril in imitation of a jug.

Bob Scobey And His Orchestra

Bob Scobey, t; Rich Matteson, b-t/tu; Jim Beebe, tb; Brian Shanley, cl; Art Hodes, p;
Clancy Hayes, bj; George Duvivier, sb; Dave Black, d.

Chicago, Ill.   7 July 1959

K2-JB-4584-5/6	Black Bottom Stomp	RCA-Victor LPM2086
K2-JB-4585-1/2	London Blues	RCA-Victor LPM2086
K2-JB-4586-4	Shake It And Break It	RCA-Victor LPM2086
K2-JB-4587-2	Canal Street Blues	RCA-Victor LPM2086

Chicago, Ill.   8 July 1959

K2-JB-4588-5	Kansas City Stomp	RCA-Victor LPM2086
K2-JB-4589-3	Buddy Bolden's Blues	RCA-Victor LPM2086
K2-JB-4590-2	Dallas Blues	RCA-Victor LPM2086
K2-JB-4591-7	Skid-Dat-De-Dat	RCA-Victor LPM2086

Chicago, Ill.   9 July 1959

K2-JB-4592-5	Fidgety Feet	RCA-Victor LPM2086
K2-JB-4593-8	The Pearls	RCA-Victor LPM2086
K2-JB-4594-8	Paging Mr. Jelly	RCA-Victor unissued
K2-JB-4595-4/6	Dukes Of Dixieland March	RCA-Victor unissued

Albert Nicholas Quartet

Albert Nicholas, cl; Art Hodes, p; Earl Murphy, sb; Freddie Kohlman, d.

Chicago, Ill.   19 July 1959

590101-9	Rose Room	Delmark DL207
590102-1	Anah's Blues	Delmark DL207
590103-1	Ain't Misbehavin'	Delmark DL207
590104-2	Etta	Delmark DL207
590105-4	I'm Coming Virginia	Delmark DL207
590106-4	Lover Come Back To Me	Delmark DL207
590107-2	Diga Diga Doo	Delmark DL207
590108-4	Winin' Boy Blues	Delmark DL207

Chicago, Ill.   27 July 1959

590103-2	Ain't Misbehavin'	Delmark unissued
590104-7	Etta	Delmark unissued
590109-3	Careless Love	Delmark unissued
590110-3	Song Of The Wanderer	Delmark DL207
590111-3	Blues My Naughty Sweetie Gives To Me	Delmark DL207

Some sources believe that the usual version of 590104 is from this session.

Albert Nicholas All Star Stompers

Nap Trottier, t; Floyd O'Brien, tb; Albert Nicholas, cl; Art Hodes, p; Marty Grosz, g;
Mike Walbridge, tu; Freddie Kohlman, d.

Chicago, Ill.   30 July 1959

590301-1	Sobbin' Blues	Delmark unissued
590302-7	Fidgety Feet	Delmark DL209
590303-4	Shimme-Sha-Wabble	Delmark DL209
590304-3	Creole Love Call	Delmark DL209

Chicago, Ill.   31 July 1959

590305-3	Gotta See Mama Every Night	Delmark DL209

590306-2/3	That's A Plenty	Delmark DL209
590307-	Farewell Blues	Delmark DL209
590308-1	Lulu's Back In Town	Delmark DL209
590309-2	How Long Blues	Delmark DL209
590310-1	Runnin' Wild	Delmark DL209

Clancy Hayes' Dixieland Band

Bobby Ballard, t; Bill Hanck, tb; Ray Daniel, cl; Art Hodes, p; Clancy Hayes, bj/v-1;
Earl Murphy, sb; Buddy Smith, d.

Chicago, Ill.   11 April 1960

Willie The Weeper -1	Audio-Fidelity AFLP1937
Careless Love -1	Audio-Fidelity AFLP1937
Original Dixieland One-Step	Audio-Fidelity AFLP1937
Nobody Knows You When You're Down And Out	Audio-Fidelity AFLP1937
Easy Street	Audio-Fidelity AFLP1937
The Blues My Naughty Sweetie Gives To Me	Audio-Fidelity AFLP1937
That's A Plenty	Audio-Fidelity unissued

Chicago, Ill.   12 April 1960

Ballin' The Jack -1	Audio-Fidelity AFLP1937
Washboard Blues -1	Audio-Fidelity AFLP1937
Baby Won't You Please Come Home-1	Audio-Fidelity AFLP1937
Sweet Georgia Brown -1	Audio-Fidelity AFLP1937
South	Audio-Fidelity unissued
I Found A New Baby	Audio-Fidelity unissued

Art Hodes's contract with Audio-Fidelity does not include the remaining two titles on
Audio-Fidelity AFLP 1937, and Art himself believes he is not on them.

Art Hodes

Art Hodes, p; Charles 'Truck' Parham, sb.

Chicago, Ill.   May 1962

24776	Randolph Street Shuffle	EmArcy MG26005
27777	Chimes Blues	EmArcy MG26005
24778	Mister Blues	EmArcy MG26005
24779	Basin Street Blues	EmArcy MG26005
24780	By A And T	EmArcy MG26005
24781	Buddy Bolden's Blues	EmArcy MG26005
24782	Call To Attention	EmArcy MG26005
24783	Washboard Blues	EmArcy MG26005
24784	Royal Garden Blues	EmArcy MG26005
24785	Snowy Morning Blues	EmArcy MG26005
24786	How Long, How Long Blues	EmArcy MG26005
24787	Pinetop's Blues	EmArcy MG26005

Mama Yancey — Art Hodes

Estella 'Mama' Yancey, v; Art Hodes, p.

Chicago, Ill.   June 1965

Good Package Blues	Verve-Folkways FVS9015
Cabbage Patch	Verve-Folkways FVS9015
Good Conductor	Verve-Folkways FVS9015
How Long Blues	Verve-Folkways FVS9015
Every Day In The Week	Verve-Folkways FVS9015

Get Him Out Of Your System	Verve-Folkways FVS9015
Sweet Lovin' Daddy	Verve-Folkways FVS9015
Trouble In Mind	Verve-Folkways FVS9015

Art Hodes, p solo.
  Same session.

Grandpa's Bells [sic]	Verve-Folkways FVS9015

Art Hodes And His All Star Stompers

Larry Conger, t; Charlie Bornemann, tb; Tony Parenti, cl; Art Hodes, p; Johnny Haines, sb; Cliff Leeman, d.
  Columbia, S.C.   8 August 1965

Cake Walkin' Babies	Jazzology J20
Shake That Thing	Jazzology J20
Strut Miss Lizzie	Jazzology J20
Willie The Weeper	Jazzology J20
Canal Street Blues	Jazzology J20
Melancholy Baby	Jazzology J20
Someday Sweetheart	Jazzology J20
California, Here I Come	Jazzology J20
Bye Bye Blues	Jazzology unissued
Blues For Buck	Jazzology unissued

Barney Bigard – Art Hodes All Star Stompers

Barney Bigard, cl; Art Hodes, p; Rail Wilson, sb; Barrett Deems, d.
  Chicago, Ill.   29 January 1968

Sweet Lorraine	Delmark DL211
Hesitation Blues	Delmark DL211
Makin' Whoopee	Delmark DL211
Three Little Words	Delmark DL211

Nap Trottier, t; George Brunis, tb/v-1; Barney Bigard, cl; Art Hodes, p; Rail Wilson, sb; Barrett Deems, d.
  Chicago, Ill.   30 January 1968

Tin Roof Blues	Delmark DL211
Tin Roof Blues (alt. take)	Delmark DS215
Sensation	Delmark DL211
Sensation (alt. take)	Delmark DS215
Bye And Bye	Delmark DL211
Bucket's Got A Hole In It -1	Delmark DL211

Art Hodes

Raymond Burke. cl; Art Hodes, p; George 'Pops' Foster, sb.
  Chicago, Ill.   22 October 1968

It's The Blues	Delmark DS213
Indiana	Delmark DS213
Steady Roll	Delmark DS213
Just A Closer Walk With Thee	Delmark DS213
Winin' Boy Blues	Delmark DS213
Do You Know What It Means To Miss New Orleans	Delmark unissued
'Neath Hawaiian Skies	Delmark unissued

	If I Could Be With You One Hour	
	Tonight	Delmark unissued
	Everybody Loves My Baby	Delmark unissued

Art Hodes With The Original New Yorkers

Bill Price, c; Jerry Mullaney, tb; Loren Helberg, cl/ts; Art Hodes, p; Biddy Bastien, sb; Bill Drake, d.

Emporium of Jazz, Mendota, Minn.   1970

	Four Or Five Times	Minnesota Jazz MJS505
	Singin' The Blues	Minnesota Jazz MJS505
	My Bucket's Got A Hole In It	Minnesota Jazz MJS505
	Gee Baby Ain't I Good To You	Minnesota Jazz MJS505
	St. Louis Blues	Minnesota Jazz MJS505
	Bye And Bye	Minnesota Jazz MJS505

Art Hodes, p solo.
  Same session.

	Washboard Blues	Minnesota Jazz MJS505

Bill Price, c; Hal Runyon, tb; Loren Helberg, cl/ts; Art Hodes, p; Dave Faison, sb; Bill Drake, d.

Emporium of Jazz, Mendota, Minn.   1970

	Sweet Georgia Brown	Minnesota Jazz MJS505
	Royal Garden Blues	Minnesota Jazz MJS505

Art Hodes

Art Hodes, p solo.
  Columbia, S.C.   5 July 1970

	Buddy Bolden's Blues	Jazzology JCE74
	Slow And Easy Man	Jazzology JCE74
	Chimes Blues	Jazzology JCE74
	Meet Me In Chicago	Jazzology JCE74
	Blues Tomorrow	Jazzology JCE74
	Miss Otis Regrets	Jazzology JCE74
	Portrait In Blue	Jazzology JCE74
	Blues Yesterday	Jazzology JCE74
	M.H. Blues	Jazzology JCE74
	Hey Mr. Yancey	Jazzology JCE74

Jens Sølund, sb-1, added.
  Copenhagen, Denmark.   5 to 10 October 1970

	Make Me A Pallet On The Floor -1	Storyville(Da) SLP215
	Blues Keep Calling -1	Storyville(Da) SLP215
	Washboard Blues	Storyville(Da) SLP215
	Organ Grinder Blues -1	Storyville(Da) SLP215
	Jackass Blues -1	Storyville(Da) SLP215
	Frankie And Johnny	Storyville(Da) SLP215
	St. Louis Blues	Storyville(Da) SLP215
	Selection From The Gutter -1	Storyville(Da) SLP215

Papa Bue's Viking Jazz Band

Jørgen Svare, cl; Art Hodes, p; Knud Ryskov Madsen, d.
  Copenhagen, Denmark.   10 October 1970

	Wolverine Blues	Storyville unissued

Finn Otto Hansen, t; Arne 'Papa' Bue Jensen, tb; Jørgen Svare, cl; Art Hodes, p; Jens
Sølund, sb; Knud Ryskov Madsen, d.
　Same session.

	Beale Street Blues	Storyville unissued
	Doctor Jazz	Storyville(Da) SLP221
	Sweet Georgia Brown	Storyville(Da) SLP425

Art Hodes, p; Knud Ryskov Madsen, d.
　Same session.

	Grandpa's Spells	Storyville(Da) SLP221

Stars Of Jazz

Wild Bill Davison, c; Jim Beebe, tb; Barney Bigard, cl; Art Hodes, p; Eddie Condon, g;
Rail Wilson, sb; Hillard Brown, d/v-1.

Pre-concert warm-up, High Point, N.C.		Fall 1971
	Kansas City Blues -1	Jazzology J62
High Point, N.C.		Fall 1971
	At The Jazz Band Ball	Jazzology J61
	Just A Closer Walk With Thee	Jazzology J61
	Tin Roof Blues	Jazzology J61
	Fidgety Feet	Jazzology J61
	Sweet Lorraine	Jazzology J62
	St. James Infirmary Blues	Jazzology J62
	Muskrat Ramble	Jazzology J62
	Farewell Blues	Jazzology J62
	Royal Garden Blues	Jazzology J62
	Blue Again	Jazzology J62
	Bill Bailey Won't You Please Come Home	Jazzology J63
	When The Saints Go Marching In	Jazzology J63
	Kansas City Blues -1	Jazzology J63

Barney Bigard, cl; Art Hodes, p; Eddie Condon, g; Rail Wilson, sb; Hillard Brown, d
　Same concerts.

	C-Jam Blues	Jazzology J63

Wild Bill Davison, c; Art Hodes, p; Rail Wilson, sb; Hillard Brown, d.
　Same concerts.

	Grandpa's Spells	Jazzology J61

Art Hodes, p; Rail Wilson, sb; Hillard Brown, d.
　Same concerts.

	Washboard Blues	Jazzology J63

Art Hodes, p; Hillard Brown, d.
　Same concerts.

	I'm Gonna Sit Right Down And Write Myself A Letter	Jazzology J63

Art Hodes, p solo
　Same concerts.

	Yancey Special	Jazzology J63

On *Grandpa's Spells* and *Sweet Lorraine*, the horns are heard only on the final notes.
Statements by the producer that these recordings were made in April 1972 are
impossible to reconcile with the known movements of the participants; the date quoted
is verified as the date of the tour during which the recordings were made.

Eddie Condon And His All Stars (FCJ141)/
Art Hodes (FCJ148)/Wallace Davenport (FCJ130)
Wild Bill Davison, c; Herb Gardner, tb-1/altoon-2; Joe Muranyi, cl; Dean Kincaide, ts-3/bar-4; Art Hodes, p; Eddie Condon, g; Van Perry, sb; Skip Tomlinson, d.

Manassas Jazz Festival, Manassas, Va.   5 December 1971

Someday You'll Be Sorry -1, 2, 3	Fat Cat's Jazz FCJ141
Avalon -1, 3, 4	Fat Cat's Jazz FCJ141
Love Is Just Around The Corner -1, 4	Fat Cat's Jazz FCJ141

Wallace Davenport, t; Herb Gardner, tb; Tommy Gwaltney, cl; Art Hodes, p; Eddie Condon, g; Van Perry, sb; Fred Moore, d.
Same concert.

Darkness On The Delta	Fat Cat's Jazz FCJ141
Milneburg Joys	Fat Cat's Jazz FCJ148

Art Hodes, p; Eddie Condon, sp.
  Same concert.

Washboard Blues	Fat Cat's Jazz FCJ141

Wallace Davenport, t; Tommy Gwaltney, cl; Art Hodes, p; Eddie Condon, g; Van Perry, sb; Fred Moore, d.
  Same concert.

St. Louis Blues No.1	Fat Cat's Jazz FCJ130

Manassas Jazz Festival 1971
Art Hodes, p; Fred Moore, wb.

Osbourn High School, Manassas, Va.   5 December 1971

Tiger Rag/Ballin' The Jack	Fat Cat's Jazz FCJ138

Wallace Davenport, t; Art Hodes, p; George 'Butch' Hall, g; Bill Goodall, sb; Fred Moore, d.
  Same concert.

Sleepy Time Down South	Fat Cat's Jazz FCJ138

Wild Bill Davison, Wild Bill Whelan, Tom Saunders, Tony Newstead, Tex Wyndham, c; John Thomas, Wallace Davenport, Kenny Fulcher, t; Spiegel Wilcox, Dick Cramer, Glen Sullivan, Walter 'Slide' Harris, Herb Gardner, tb; Herb Hall, Tommy Gwaltney, Jim Weaver, Larry Kopp, Joe Muranyi, cl; Deane Kincaide, ts; Art Hodes, Jean Kittrell, Rick Cordrey, John Eaton, Johnny Wiggin, Jean Griffin, p; Bud Ahern, Jerry Addicott, bj; George 'Butch' Hall, Steve Jordan, Eddie Condon, g; Rolf Dahlen, helicon; Bill Goodall, Van Perry, sb; Fred Moore, Skip Tomlinson, Ken Underwood, d; Jay Rosenthal, wb.
  Same concert.

Strutting With Some	
Bar-B-Q (Finale)	Fat Cat's Jazz FCJ138

The 'ride out' on this title is said to involve all the musicians participating in the concert, but it is impossible to know how seriously to take this. Dan Simms has reported that even after discussions with Johnson 'Fat Cat' McRee in 1988, it was impossible to be sure of the composition of the rhythm section. All those heard on the double album Fat Cat's Jazz FCJ137/138 are noted above; all the listed cornetists and trumpeters, Herb Hall, and Art Hodes are confirmed to take part.

Joe Muranyi
Dick Sudhalter, c; Danny Williams, tb; Joe Muranyi, cl/v-1; Art Hodes, p; Van Perry, sb; Bob Thompson, d.

prob. Manassas Jazz Festival, Manassas, Va.   prob. December 1971

The Love Nest	Fat Cat's Jazz FCJ198
Poor Butterfly	Fat Cat's Jazz FCJ198

Love Is Just Around The Corner	Fat Cat's Jazz FCJ198
Singin' The Blues	Fat Cat's Jazz FCJ198
New Orleans	Fat Cat's Jazz FCJ198
Swing That Music -1	Fat Cat's Jazz FCJ198

The date and place of recording of this session is not definitely confirmed.

Art Hodes

Art Hodes, p; Charles 'Truck' Parham, sb; Barrett Deems, d.

Chicago, Ill.   16 March 1972

Real Thing	Delmark unissued
You Gotta Give Me Some	Delmark unissued
Tin Roof Blues	Delmark unissued
Basin Street Blues	Delmark unissued
Watermelon Man	Delmark unissued
Blues Yesterday	Delmark DS213
Winin' Boy Blues	Delmark DS213
New Orleans/Sleepy Time Down South	Delmark unissued
Old Fashioned Love	Delmark DS213
St. Louis Blues	Delmark unissued
Ballin' The Jack	Delmark unissued

Voltaire 'Volly' DeFaut, cl; Art Hodes, p; Charles 'Truck' Parham, sb; Barrett Deems, d.

Chicago, Ill.   23 March 1972

Struttin' With Some Barbecue	Delmark DS213
That's A Plenty	Delmark DS215
After You've Gone	Delmark unissued
Sleepy Time Down South	Delmark unissued
I Know That You Know	Delmark unissued
Jackass Blues	Delmark unissued
Bye Bye Blues	Delmark unissued

Art Hodes

Art Hodes, p solo.

University of Southern Illinois, Edwardsville, Ill.   13 April 1972

Grandpa's Spells	Euphonic ESR1207
Hesitation Blues	Euphonic ESR1207
The Smootch	Euphonic ESR1207
Closer Walk With Thee	Euphonic ESR1207
Blues Yesterday	Euphonic ESR1207
Ballin' The Jack	Euphonic ESR1207
Pagin' Mr. Jelly	Euphonic ESR1207
Dear Old Southland	Euphonic ESR1207
Tin Roof Blues	Euphonic ESR1207
Watermelon Man	Euphonic ESR1207
St. James Infirmary	Euphonic ESR1207
Oh, Baby, Please Don't Go	Euphonic ESR1207
The Saints	Euphonic ESR1207

Art Hodes

Nap Trottier, t; George Brunis, tb/v-1; Voltaire 'Volly' DeFaut, cl; Art Hodes, p; Charles 'Truck' Parham, sb; Barrett Deems, d.

Chicago, Ill.   25 April 1972

Clarinet Marmalade	Delmark DS215

Angry -1	Delmark DS215
Sobbin' Blues	Delmark DS215
Panama	Delmark DS215
Ja Da	Delmark DS215
When My Sugar Walks Down	
The Street	Delmark DS213
NORK Blues	Delmark DS215

Big Horn Jazz Fest '72

Wild Bill Davison, George Brunis, tb/nose-1/v-2/sp-3; Bob Wilber, cl-4/ss-5; Art Hodes, p; Rail Wilson, sb; Barrett Deems, d; Eddie Condon, sp-6.

Big Horn Jazz Festival, Ivanhoe, Ill. 29 May 1972

Avalon -5, 6	Big Horn SB2001
Tin Roof Blues -1, 2, 3, 5, 6	Big Horn SB2001
Muskrat Ramble -3, 4, 6	Big Horn SB2001
Sweet Georgia Brown -4, 6	Big Horn SB2001

Muskrat Ramble is announced as *Mousetrap Strangle*.

Wallace Davenport

Wallace Davenport, t; Walter 'Slide' Harris, tb; Wally Garner, cl; Art Hodes, p; Van Perry, sb; Freddie Moore, d.

Manassas Jazz Festival, Manassas, Va. 2 December 1972

Tin Roof Blues	Fat Cat's Jazz FCJ130
Is It True What They Say About Dixie?	Fat Cat's Jazz FCJ130

Tony Newstead

Tony Newstead, c; Danny Williams, tb; Mason 'Country' Thomas, cl; Art Hodes, p; Danny Barker, g; Frank Tate, sb; Freddie Moore, d.

Manassas Jazz Festival, Manassas, Va. 2 December 1972

Royal Garden Blues	Fat Cat's Jazz FCJ127

Johnny Wiggs Bayou Stompers

Johnny Wiggs, c; Bill Allred, tb; Raymond Burke, cl; Art Hodes, p; George 'Butch' Hall, g; Van Perry, sb; Cliff Leeman, d; Johnson 'Fat Cat' McRee, v-1.

Manassas Jazz Festival, Manassas, Va. 2 December 1972

City Of A Million Dreams	Fat Cat's Jazz FCJ129
Louisiana	Fat Cat's Jazz FCJ129
New Orleans	Fat Cat's Jazz FCJ129
I'll Be A Friend With Pleasure -1	Fat Cat's Jazz FCJ129

Art Hodes

Tony Newstead, c; Danny Williams, tb; Mason 'Country' Thomas, cl; Art Hodes, p; Danny Barker, g; Bill Goodall, sb; Frank Marshall, d.

Manassas, Va. 2 December 1972

Ballin' The Jack	Fat Cat's Jazz FCJ148
'Way Down Yonder In N.O. [*sic*]	Fat Cat's Jazz FCJ148

Wild Bill Davison, c; Danny Williams, tb; Tommy Gwaltney, cl; Art Hodes, p; Steve Jordan, g; Bill Goodall, sb; Cliff Leeman, d.

Manassas, Va. 3 December 1972

Avalon	Fat Cat's Jazz FCJ148

Do You Know What It Mean To Miss
N.O. [*sic*]   Fat Cat's Jazz FCJ148

Wild Bill Davison And Tommy Saunders
Wild Bill Davison, c-2; Tommy Saunders, c/v-1; Danny Williams, tb; Jack Maheu, cl;
Art Hodes, p; Danny Barker, g; Frank Tate, sb; Ken Underwood, d.
   Manassas Jazz Festival, Manassas, Va.   3 December 1972
       I Never Knew -2   Fat Cat's Jazz FCJ134
       Someday You'll Be Sorry -1, 2   Fat Cat's Jazz FCJ134
       There'll Be Some Changes Made   Fat Cat's Jazz FCJ134
       Wolverine Blues   Fat Cat's Jazz FCJ134
The exact instrumentation of the two titles without Wild Bill Davison is not confirmed.

Manassas Jazz Festival 1972
Wild Bill Davison, c; Danny Williams, tb; Tom Gwaltney, cl; Art Hodes, p; Steve
Jordan, g; Bill Goodall, sb; Cliff Leeman, d.
   Stonewall Jackson High School, Manassas, Va.   2 December 1972
       Fidgety Feet   Fat Cat's Jazz FCJ143
Tony Newstead, c; Danny Williams, tb; Mason 'Country' Thomas, cl; Art Hodes, p;
Danny Barker, g; Bill Goodall, sb; Frank Marshall, d.
   Manassas Jazz Festival, Manassas, Va.   December 1972
       St. James Infirmary   Fat Cat's Jazz FCJ143/144
Johnny Wiggs, Wild Bill Davison, Tony Newstead, Tom Saunders, c; Wallace
Davenport, Kenny Fulcher, t; Bill Allred, Danny Williams, Graham Stewart, tb;
Raymond Burke, Tom Gwaltney, Mason 'Country' Thomas, Jack Maheu, Wally Garner,
cl; Ray Whittam, bsx; Art Hodes, Claude Hopkins, Bob Greene, Charles 'Tex'
Wyndham, John Eaton, p; Danny Barker, Steve Jordan, George 'Butch' Hall, g; Bill
Goodall, Van Perry, Frank Tate, sb; Cliff Leeman, Fred Moore, Frank Marshall, Skip
Tomlinson, d.
   Same concerts.
       Blues Finale   Fat Cat's Jazz FCJ143/144
This title is said to involve all the musicians who participated in the 1972 Manassas
Jazz Festival, but it is impossible to know how seriously to take this, or whether the
names cited are a complete list of participants!
The Manassas Jazz Festival 1972 was recorded at Stonewall Jackson High School and
Osbourn High School, Manassas, Va., on 2 December 1972, and at Marshall Aviation
Hangar, Manassas Municipal Airport, Manassas, Va., on 3 December 1972, but no
information is available as to which titles were recorded at which locations or on which
date, except as shown. These locations and dates will presumably apply to other Fat
Cat's Jazz albums recorded at the 1972 Manassas Jazz Festival.

Ernie Carson
Collective personnel: Ernie Carson, c; Bill Allred, Bill Rank, Al Winters, tb; Jack
Maheu, Herbie Hall, cl; Kenny Davern, George Probert, ss; Spencer Clark, bsx; Bob
Hirsch, Art Hodes, p; George Hall, g; Van Perry, Stan Booth, sb; Bill Goodall, eb; Cliff
Leeman, Roger Davidson, d.
   Manassas, Va.   December 1973
       Dinah   Fat Cat's Jazz FCJ164
       Battle Hymn Of The Republic   Fat Cat's Jazz FCJ164
       Jelly Roll   Fat Cat's Jazz FCJ164
       Clarinet Marmalade   Fat Cat's Jazz FCJ164
Art Hodes may not be present on all the above; titles on this album on which it is
known that Claude Hopkins is the pianist are omitted.

Doc Evans (FCJ178)/Art Hodes (FCJ148)

Paul 'Doc' Evans, t; Al Winters, tb; Mason 'Country' Thomas, cl; Spencer Clark, bsx;
Art Hodes, p; Van Perry, sb; Skip Tomlinson, d.

Ramada Inn, Manassas, Va.   1 December 1973
      Wolverine Blues   Fat Cat's Jazz FCJ178
      When My Sugar Walks Down
      The Street   Fat Cat's Jazz FCJ178
      Hesitation Blues   Fat Cat's Jazz FCJ178
      Bye And Bye   Fat Cat's Jazz FCJ148

Art Hodes

Art Hodes, p solo.

Manassas Jazz Festival, Manassas, Va.   1 December 1973
      Miss Otis Regrets   Fat Cat's Jazz FCJ148

1973 Manassas Jazz Festival

Johnny Wiggs, c; Walter 'Slide' Harris, tb; Herbie Hall, cl; Art Hodes, p; George 'Butch'
Hall, g; Frank Tate, sb; Skip Tomlinson, d; Johnson 'Fat Cat' McRee, v.

Manassas Jazz Festival, Osbourn High School, Manassas, Va.   1 December 1973
      Just A Gigolo   Fat Cat's Jazz FCJ172

Art Hodes

Art Hodes, p solo.

Manassas Jazz Festival, Manassas, Va.   2 December 1973
      Washboard Blues   Fat Cat's Jazz FCJ148
      Blues Yesterday, Today And Tomorrow Fat Cat's Jazz FCJ148

Natalie Lamb

Kenny Davern, cl; Art Hodes, p; Jerry Addicott, bj; Van Perry, sb; Bob Thompson, d;
Natalie Lamb, v.

Manassas Jazz Festival, Manassas, Va.,   2 December 1973
      If You Lose Your Money Blues   Fat Cat's Jazz FCJ152
      Got Me Goin' and Close   Fat Cat's Jazz FCJ152

Art Hodes And His Down Home Jazz Band

Ernie Carson, c; Charlie Bornemann, tb; Franz Jackson, cl-1/ss-2/ts-3/v-4; Art Hodes,
p; Jimmy Johnson, sb/whistling-6; Hillard Brown, d/v-5.

Atlanta, Ga.   31 October 1974
      Joshua Fit De Battle Of Jericho -1, 6   Jazzology J58
      Buddy Bolden's Blues -1   Jazzology J58
      Hey Now, Let's Have Some Fun
      Tonight -3, 5   Jazzology J58
      Dixie -1, 2   Jazzology J58
      Back Home Again In Indiana -1   Jazzology J58
      Oh Didn't He Ramble -2, 4   Jazzology J58
      Taking It Easy -1   Jazzology J58
      Chicago -2   Jazzology J58
      Somebody's Got To Go -2, 5   Jazzology J58
      Washington And Lee Swing -1, 3   Jazzology J58

The band credit is as shown on the label of Jazzology J58; the sleeve gives the credit as
'Art Hodes Jazz Four...Plus Two'.

Doc Evans

Collective personnel: Paul 'Doc' Evans, t; Bill Allred, Al Winters, tb; Tommy Gwaltney, Wally Garner, cl; Spencer Clark, bsx; Art Hodes, Bobby Hirsch, p; George 'Butch' Hall, g; Van Perry, Bill Goodall, Gene Mayl, sb; Skip Tomlinson, d.

Manassas Jazz Festival, Manassas, Va.,   December 1975

I Can't Believe That You're In Love With Me	Fat Cat's Jazz FCJ185
Blue Turning Grey Over You	Fat Cat's Jazz FCJ185
Jelly Roll	Fat Cat's Jazz FCJ185
Blue And Brokenhearted	Fat Cat's Jazz FCJ185
Struttin' With Some Bar-B-Q	Fat Cat's Jazz FCJ185
Buddy Bolden Blues	Fat Cat's Jazz FCJ185
Just A Closer Walk With Thee	Fat Cat's Jazz FCJ185

It is unlikely that Art Hodes is present on all titles on this album, but full details have not been available.

It is likely that some at least of these titles were recorded at the 6 December 1975 Doc Evans session listed below.

Max Kaminsky

Max Kaminsky, t; Al Winters, tb; Tommy Gwaltney, cl; Spencer Clark, bsx; Art Hodes, p; George 'Butch' Hall, g; Gene Mayl, sb; Skip Tomlinson, d.

Manassas Jazz Festival, Manassas, Va.,   6 December 1975

I Wish I Could Shimmy Like My Sister Kate	Fat Cat's Jazz FCJ206

Maxine Sullivan

Wally Garner, cl; Art Hodes, p; George 'Butch' Hall, g; Van Perry, Gene Mayl, sb; Bob Thompson, d; Maxine Sullivan, v.

All Saints Church Auditorium, Manassas, Va.   6 December 1975

I'm Comin' Virginia	Fat Cat's Jazz FCJ195

Doc Evans

Paul 'Doc' Evans, t; Al Winters, tb; Wally Garner, cl; Spencer Clark, bsx; Art Hodes, p; Bill Goodall, eb; Skip Tomlinson, d.

All Saints Catholic Church Auditorium, Manassas, Va.   6 December 1975

Save It Pretty Mama	Fat Cat's Jazz FCJ178

See also Fat Cat's Jazz FCJ185 above.

Art Hodes

Art Hodes, p solos.

Wayne Stahnke's house, Santa Monica, Cal.   19 September 1976

Baby, Won't You Please Come Home?	Euphonic ESR1213
Alexander's Ragtime Band	Euphonic ESR1213
You've Got To Give Me Some	Euphonic ESR1213
Yonder Come The Blues	Euphonic ESR1213
Cakewalkin' Babies From Home	Euphonic ESR1213
Backwater Blues	Euphonic ESR1213
Nobody Knows You When You're Down And Out	Euphonic ESR1213
Georgia Cakewalk (At A Georgia Camp Meeting)	Euphonic ESR1213
You've Been A Good Old Wagon	Euphonic ESR1213

Slow And Easy Man	Euphonic ESR1213
Yellow Dog Blues	Euphonic ESR1213
A Good Man Is Hard To Find	Euphonic ESR1213

London.   26 to 30 June 1977

Chimes Blues	un-numbered cassette (E)
Battle Hymn Of The Republic	un-numbered cassette (E)
Gonna Sit Right Down And Write	
Myself A Letter	un-numbered cassette (E)
Grandpa's Spells	un-numbered cassette (E)
Plain Ol' Blues	un-numbered cassette (E)
The Saints	un-numbered cassette (E)
You Are My Sunshine	un-numbered cassette (E)
Salute To Basie	un-numbered cassette (E)
Watermelon Man	un-numbered cassette (E)
I Can't Get Started	un-numbered cassette (E)
Limehouse Blues	un-numbered cassette (E)
Sunny Side Of The Street	un-numbered cassette (E)
Sweet Georgia Brown	un-numbered cassette (E)
Miss Otis Regrets	un-numbered cassette (E)
Gone Away Blues	un-numbered cassette (E)
St. Louis Blues	un-numbered cassette (E)
Maryland My Maryland	un-numbered cassette (E)
Pinetop's Blues	un-numbered cassette (E)

This cassette, which has no label name or issue number, was sold during Art Hodes's 1988 British tour.

Maxine Sullivan

Ernie Carson, c; Jack Howe, ts; Spencer Clark, bsx; Art Hodes, p; John Haynes, sb; Tom Martin, d; Maxine Sullivan, v.

Columbia, S.C.   6 February 1978

I Got A Right To Sing The Blues	Audiophile AP128
Exactly Like You	Audiophile AP128
Someday Sweetheart	Audiophile AP128
You Were Meant For Me	Audiophile AP128
Miss Otis Regrets	Audiophile AP128
We Just Couldn't Say Goodbye	Audiophile AP128
The Devil And The Deep Blue Sea	Audiophile AP128
St. Louis Blues	Audiophile AP128
That Old Feeling	Audiophile AP128
I'm Gonna Sit Right Down And	
Write Myself A Letter	Audiophile AP128

Art Hodes, p; John Haynes, sb; Tom Martin, d; Maxine Sullivan, v.

Same session.

Legalize My Name	Audiophile AP128
He's Funny That Way	Audiophile AP128

Art Hodes And His Chicagoans

Ernie Carson, c; Charlie Bornemann, tb; Herman Foretich, cl; Spencer Clark, bsx; Art Hodes, p; Jerry Rousseau, sb; Spider Ridgway, d.

Columbia, S.C.   7 February 1978

This Could Be My Lucky Day	Jazzology J79
It's The Talk Of The Town	Jazzology J79

Makin' Whoopee	Jazzology J79
Sunday	Jazzology J79
You're Driving Me Crazy	Jazzology J79
Love Nest	Jazzology J79
Walkin' My Baby Back Home	Jazzology J79
'Posin' [*sic*]	Jazzology J79
'S' Wonderful [*sic*]	Jazzology J79

The band credit is as shown on the label of Jazzology J79; the sleeve gives the credit as
'Art Hodes And His Windy City Seven'.

Art Hodes

Art Hodes, p solos.

Wayne Stahnke's house, Venice, Cal. 23 May 1978

Cherry	Euphonic ESR1218
Gee, Baby Ain't I Good To You	Euphonic ESR1218
I Know That You Know	Euphonic ESR1218
I'm Coming Virginia	Euphonic ESR1218
Blue Turning Grey Over You	Euphonic ESR1218
Judy	Euphonic ESR1218
Save It Pretty Mama	Euphonic ESR1218
Truckin'	Euphonic ESR1218
Georgia On My Mind	Euphonic ESR1218
Mood Indigo	Euphonic ESR1218
The Mooche	Euphonic unissued
Pallet On The Floor	Euphonic unissued
Chimes Blues	Euphonic unissued
St. Louis Blues	Euphonic unissued
After You've Gone	Euphonic unissued
Down Home Blues	Euphonic unissued
Up A Lazy River	Euphonic unissued
Someday, Sweetheart	Euphonic unissued
Apex Blues	Euphonic unissued
Sweet Georgia Brown	Euphonic unissued
Washboard Blues	Euphonic unissued
Just A Closer Walk With Thee	Euphonic unissued
Do You Know What It Means To Miss New Orleans	Euphonic unissued
Yellow Dog Blues	Euphonic unissued
Maryland, My Maryland	Euphonic unissued
Boy In The Boat (Squeeze Me)	Euphonic unissued
Farewell Blues	Euphonic unissued
Jackass Blues	Euphonic unissued
Tin Roof Blues	Euphonic unissued
Royal Garden Blues	Euphonic unissued
Limehouse Blues	Euphonic unissued
Plain Old Blues	Euphonic unissued
St. James Infirmary	Euphonic unissued
Struttin' With Some Barbecue	Euphonic unissued

Art Hodes Blue Six

Sammy Duncan, c; Charlie Bornemann, tb; Herman Foretich, cl; Art Hodes, p; Peter
Himmage, sb; Duncan Souter, d.

The Sound Pit, Atlanta, Ga.   October 1978

Blues Groove	Jazzology J155
Mama's Gone Goodbye	Jazzology J155
When My Dreamboat Comes Home	Jazzology J155
Royal Garden Blues	Jazzology J155
Mornin' After Blues	Jazzology J155
Blue Skies	Jazzology J155
Lazy Bones	Jazzology J155
Farewell Blues	Jazzology J155

The Hot Three
Kenny Davern, cl; Art Hodes, p; Dominick 'Dom' DeMichael, d.
The Great Hall, St. John's University, Annapolis, Md.   1 July 1979

Fidgety Feet	Monmouth-Evergreen MES7091
Chimes Blues	Monmouth-Evergreen MES7091
Shim-Me-Sha-Wabble	Monmouth-Evergreen MES7091
Liberty Inn Drag	Monmouth-Evergreen MES7091
Some Of These Days	Monmouth-Evergreen MES7091
Ballin' The Jack	Monmouth-Evergreen MES7091
See See Rider	Monmouth-Evergreen MES7091
It Don't Mean A Thing	Monmouth-Evergreen MES7091
My Blue Heaven	Monmouth-Evergreen MES7091

Art Hodes, p solo.
Same session.

Tennessee Waltz	Monmouth-Evergreen MES7091

Art Hodes
Art Hodes, p solos.
Hanratty's Club, New York City.   27 February 1981

Selection From The Gutter	Muse MR5252
Liza	Muse MR5252
Exactly Like You	Muse MR5252
Grandpa's Spells	Muse MR5252
Someone To Watch Over Me	Muse MR5252
St. Louis Blues	Muse MR5252
Georgia On My Mind	Muse MR5252
Sweet Georgia Brown	Muse MR5252
Save It Pretty Mama	Muse MR5252
Plain Ol' Blues	Muse MR5252
Washboard Blues	Muse MR5252
Struttin' With Some Barbecue	Muse MR5252

Art Hodes with Milt Hinton
Art Hodes, p; Milt Hinton, sb.
The Cabbage Patch, New York City.   26 August 1981

Willow Weep For Me	Muse MR5279
Winin'	Muse MR5279
I Would Do Most Anything	Muse MR5279
Low Down N' Below	Muse MR5279
Bye & Bye	Muse MR5279
Down Home Blues	Muse MR5279

Randolph Street Blues	Muse MR5279
Here Comes Cow Cow	Muse MR5279
Miss Otis Regrets	Muse MR5279
Milt Jumps	Muse MR5279

Art Hodes International Trio

Reimer von Essen, cl; Art Hodes, p; Trevor Richards, d.

Amerika Haus, Frankfurt-am-Main, Germany	3 November 1981
& Audio-Lab Tonstudio, Oberursel, Germany	8 November 1981
How Long Blues	L&R(G) LR40015
Careless Love	L&R(G) LR40015
Blues My Naughty Sweetie Gives	
To Me	L&R(G) LR40015
Cow Cow Blues	L&R(G) LR40015
Blues To Save The Trees	L&R(G) LR40015
Old Fashioned Love	L&R(G) LR40015
Old Rugged Cross	L&R(G) LR40015

Art Hodes, p solos.
  Same sessions.

Mamie's Blues	L&R(G) LR40015
Play No Blues	L&R(G) LR40015

It is not known which titles on the above album were recorded at which of the two quoted sessions; the locations may possibly be reversed to dates.

Art Hodes And The Red Hot Pods

Dieter Bietack, t; Harry Jirsa, tb; Claus Nemeth, cl/ss/ts; Art Hodes, p; Erwin Frassine, bj; Bibi Libowitzky, sb; Leopold Mayer, d.

Vienna, Austria.	26 October 1982
Gatemouth	Groove(As) 0650
Buddy Bolden Blues	Groove(As) 0650
Shine	Groove(As) 0650
Darling Nelly Gray	Groove(As) 0650
Mood Indigo	Groove(As) 0650

Lothar Reichhold, bj, replaces Frassine.
  Same session.

Panama	Groove(As) 0650

Art Hodes, p solo.
  Same session.

Struttin' With Some Barbecue	Groove(As) 0650
Gone Away Blues	Groove(As) 0650
Jazzland	Groove(As) 0650
Pagin' Mr. Jelly	Groove(As) 0650

The Magnolia Jazz Band & Art Hodes (171)/
Art Hodes & The Magnolia Jazz Band (172)

Jim Borkenhagen, t; Jim Klippert, tb; Bill Carter, cl; Art Hodes, p; Dan Ruedger, bj/v; Robbie Schlosser, sb; Jeff Hamilton, d.

Stanford, Cal.	January 1983
See See Rider	G.H.B. GHB171
Yearning	G.H.B. GHB171
Life Is Like A Book	G.H.B. GHB171
Weary Blues	G.H.B. GHB171

Chimes Blues	G.H.B. GHB171	
Ain't Gonna Give Nobody None		
Of My Jelly Roll	G.H.B. GHB171	
Someday Sweetheart	G.H.B. GHB171	
Shake That Thing	G.H.B. GHB171	
How Long, How Long Blues	G.H.B. GHB172	
Just A Little While To Stay Here	G.H.B. GHB172	
Hurry Down Sunshine	G.H.B. GHB172	
Linger Awhile	G.H.B. GHB172	
Magnolia Blues	G.H.B. GHB172	
Some Of These Days	G.H.B. GHB172	
Beale Street Blues	G.H.B. GHB172	
I'm Looking Over A Four-Leaf Clover	G.H.B. GHB172	

Art Hodes

Art Hodes, p solo.
Toronto, Ont.   29 November 1983

South Side Memories	Sackville(Ca) 3032
Melancholy	Sackville(Ca) 3032
Savoy Blues	Sackville(Ca) 3032
London Blues	Sackville(Ca) 3032
Cakewalkin' Babies From Home	Sackville(Ca) 3032
Mamie's Blues	Sackville(Ca) 3032
Willie The Weeper	Sackville(Ca) 3032
The Pearls	Sackville(Ca) 3032
I Know That You Know	Sackville(Ca) 3032
Blues Keep Callin'	Sackville(Ca) 3032
It's A Happening	Sackville(Ca) 3032

Avondale Estate, Ga.   13 July 1984

Does Jesus Love Me?	Jazzology JCE93
Old Time Religion	Jazzology JCE93
Swing Low, Sweet Chariot	Jazzology JCE93
Bye And Bye	Jazzology JCE93
Just A Closer Walk With Thee	Jazzology JCE93
Nobody Knows The Trouble I've Seen	Jazzology JCE93
Joshua Fit The Battle Of Jericho	Jazzology JCE93
Just A Little While To Stay Here	Jazzology JCE93

The Authentic Art Hodes Rhythm Section accompanies Carrie Smith with Doc Cheatham

Doc Cheatham, t; Art Hodes, p; Carrie Smith, v
New York City.   7 June 1985

Back Water Blues	Parkwood (Ca) PW106
Maybe Not At All (Not On The	
First Night Baby)	Parkwood (Ca) PW106
Wasted Life Blues	Parkwood (Ca) PW106
Big Butter And Egg Man	Parkwood (Ca) PW106

Doc Cheatham, t; Art Hodes, p.
New York City.   8 June 1985

Jelly Roll Blues	Parkwood(Ca) PW106
When It's Sleepy Time Down South	Parkwood(Ca) PW106

Carrie Smith, v, added.
  Same session.

You Rascal You (I'll Be Glad When You're Dead)	Parkwood(Ca) PW106
There'll Be Some Changes Made	Parkwood(Ca) PW106

Art Hodes
Art Hodes, p solo.
  McClear Place, Toronto, Ont.   16 June 1985

Blues In The Night	Sackville(Ca) 3039
Pennies From Heaven	Sackville(Ca) 3039
Morning Comes Morning Goes	Sackville(Ca) 3039
Lazybones	Sackville(Ca) 3039
Snowball	Sackville(Ca) 3039
Please Don't Talk About Me When I'm Gone	Sackville(Ca) 3039
A Ghost Of A Chance	Sackville(Ca) 3039
Summertime	Sackville(Ca) 3039

O'Shaugnessy Auditorium, College of St. Catherine, St. Paul, Minn. 29 June 1985

unknown titles	K-Twin # unknown
	[NTSC video (1)]

Art Hodes and Bud Freeman
Bud Freeman, ts; Art Hodes, p; Biddy Bastien, sb; Hal Smith, d.
  Same concert.

Ain't Misbehavin'	K-Twin # unknown
	[NTSC video (1)]
unknown titles	K-Twin # unknown
	[NTSC video (2)]

Art Hodes
Art Hodes, p solo.
  Civic Hall, Ballarat, Vic.   27 December 1985

Blues	Eureka Jazz(Au) DEX126E
Tribute To Fats	Eureka Jazz(Au) DEX126E

John McCarthy, cl; Art Hodes, p; Allan Browne, d.
  Same concert.

Beale St. Blues	Eureka Jazz(Au) DEX126E
Darktown Strutter's Ball	Eureka Jazz(Au) DEX126E

Art Hodes, p solo.
  Civic Hall, Ballarat, Vic.   29 December 1985

42nd Street	Eureka Jazz(Au) DEX126E
When I Grow Too Old To Dream	Eureka Jazz(Au) DEX126E

Art Hodes, Jan Hodes, p duet (at one p).
  Same concert.

Salute To Cow Cow	Eureka Jazz(Au) DEX126E

Neville Stribling, cl; Ade Monsbourgh, as; Art Hodes, p; Peter Gallen, sb; Allan Browne, d.
  Same concert.

Monday Date	Eureka Jazz(Au) DEX126E

Fred Parkes, cl; Art Hodes, p; John Scurry, g; John Bartlett, sb; Allan Browne, d.
Civic Hall, Ballarat, Vic.   30 December 1985
    Lady Be Good   Eureka Jazz(Au) DEX126E
    Muskrat Ramble   Eureka Jazz(Au) DEX126E

Fred Parkes, cl; Art Hodes, p; Allan Browne, d.
Civic Hall, Ballarat, Vic.   31 December 1985
    I Would Do Most Anything For You Eureka Jazz(Au) DEX126E
John McCarthy, Fred Parkes, cl; Art Hodes, p; Allan Browne, d.
Same concert.
    Memphis Blues   Eureka Jazz(Au) DEX126E

Chicago Jazz Summit

Max Kaminsky, t; George Masso, tb; Clarence Hutchenrider, cl; Eddie Miller, ts; Art
Hodes, p; Ikey Robinson, bj; Vince Giordano, bsx.
Town Hall, New York City.   22 June 1986
    Sweet Georgia Brown   Atlantic Jazz 7-81844-2 [CD]
Art Hodes, p solo.
Same session.
    St. Louis Blues   Atlantic Jazz 7-81844-2 [CD]
Wild Bill Davison, c; George Masso, tb; Kenny Davern, cl; Franz Jackson, ts/v-1; Art
Hodes, p; Vince Giordano, g; Milt Hinton, sb; Barrett Deems, d.
Same session.
    Blue Turning Grey Over You Atlantic Jazz 7-81844-2 [CD]
    When You're Smiling -1   Atlantic Jazz 7-81844-2 [CD]
The liner notes credit the vocal on When You're Smiling incorrectly to Wild Bill
Davison; Vince Giordano has stated that it is by Jackson.

Art Hodes

Art Hodes, p solo.
Moot Court Auditorium, University of Windsor, Ont.   20 April 1987
    Greensleeves (What Child Is This?) Parkwood(Ca) PW108
    Silent Night   Parkwood(Ca) PW108
    White Christmas   Parkwood(Ca) PW108
    Joy To The World   Parkwood(Ca) PW108
    Jingle Bells   Parkwood(Ca) PW108

Moot Court Auditorium, University of Windsor, Ont.   18 June 1987
    Away In A Manger   Parkwood(Ca) PW108
    Hark! The Herald Angels Sing Parkwood(Ca) PW108
    We Wish You A Merry Christmas Parkwood(Ca) PW108

Art Hodes

Pat Halcox, t; Wally Fawkes, cl; Art Hodes, p; Andy Brown, sb; Dave Evans, d.
Acton, London.   26 September 1987
    I Want A Little Girl   Jazzology JCD172 [CD]
    Willie The Weeper   Jazzology JCD172 [CD]
    Salty Dog   Jazzology JCD172 [CD]
    Doctor Jazz   Jazzology JCD172 [CD]
    Trouble In Mind   Jazzology unissued
Pat Halcox, t; Art Hodes, p; Andy Brown, sb; Dave Evans, d.

Same session.

Wrap Your Troubles In Dreams	Jazzology JCD172 [CD]

Al Fairweather, t; Art Hodes, p; Fapy Lapertin, g; Andy Brown, sb; Stan Greig, d;
Johnny Mars, v-1/h-1.

Acton, London.   6 October 1987

Trouble In Mind -1	Jazzology JCD172 [CD]
Canal Street Blues	Jazzology JCD172 [CD]
Old Stack O'Lee Blues	Jazzology JCD172 [CD]
(I Had) A Date With An Angel -1	Jazzology JCD172 [CD]
When You And I Were Young Maggie	Jazzology unissued

Art Hodes, p; Andy Brown, sb.

Same session.

Squeeze Me	Jazzology JCD172 [CD]
Tin Roof Blues	Jazzology JCD172 [CD]

Art Hodes, p solo.

Same session.

A Little Bit Of Yancey In London	Jazzology JCD172 [CD]

Tin Roof Blues was recorded as *Shake That Thing*.

The Art Hodes — John Petters Hot Three

Trevor Whiting, cl-1/ss-2/as-3; Art Hodes, p; John Petters, d; Dave Bennett, v-4.

London.   9 October 1987

Clarinet Marmalade -1	Jazz(E) JC005 [cassette]
Lazybones -1	Jazz(E) JC005 [cassette]
Mama's Gone, Goodbye -3	Jazz(E) JC005 [cassette]
Lonesome Blues -2	Jazz(E) JC005 [cassette]
Jackass Blues -2	CMJ(E) CD007 [CD]
Cake Walking Babies -1	Jazz(E) JC005 [cassette]
Sensation Rag -1	Jazz(E) JC005 [cassette]
Jeep's Blues -2	Jazz(E) JC005 [cassette]
Balling The Jack -1, 4	Jazz(E) JC005 [cassette]
Snowball	Jazz(E) JC005 [cassette]
Dear Old Southland -2	CMJ(E) CD007 [CD]
Wolverine Blues -1	Jazz(E) JC005 [cassette]

All titles from this session are on CMJ CD007.

Art Hodes & Marcus Belgrave

Marcus Belgrave, t; Art Hodes, p.

Moot Court Auditorium, University of Windsor, Ont.   23 February 1988

Watermelon Man	Parkwood(Ca) PW113 [cassette]
Do You Know What It Means	
(To Miss New Orleans)	Parkwood(Ca) PW113 [cassette]
She's Funny That Way	Parkwood(Ca) PW113 [cassette]
September Song	Parkwood(Ca) PW113 [cassette]

Art Hodes And His Blues Serenaders

Abbi Hubner, c; Reimer von Essen, cl; Art Hodes, p; Trevor Richards, d.

Frankfurt-am-Main, Germany.   17 April 1988

Too Sweet For Words	Stomp Off SOS1184
Mojo Blues	Stomp Off SOS1184
Heebie Jeebies	Stomp Off SOS1184

In The Alley Blues	Stomp Off SOS1184
Traveling Blues	Stomp Off SOS1184
Peepin' Blues	Stomp Off SOS1184
Steppin' On The Blues	Stomp Off SOS1184
Charleston Mad	Stomp Off SOS1184
Rampart Street Blues	Stomp Off SOS1184
Blues For Lovie Austin	Stomp Off SOS1184
Galion Stomp	Stomp Off SOS1184

Art Hodes

Art Hodes, p solo.

Acton, London.   5 May 1988

-1	Trouble In Mind	Dawn Club(E) 77-10
-1	Blues Keep Calling	Dawn Club(E) 77-10
-1	Black & Blue	Dawn Club(E) 77-10
-1	Forty Second Street	Dawn Club(E) 77-10
-1	Atlanta Blues	Dawn Club(E) 77-10
-1	Organ Grinder Blues	Dawn Club(E) 77-10
-1	Old Fashioned Love	Dawn Club(E) 77-10
-1	Lonesome Blues	Dawn Club(E) 77-10
-1	Bye & Bye	Dawn Club(E) 77-10
-2	Aunt Hagar's Blues	Dawn Club(E) 77-10
-1	I'm Coming Virginia	Dawn Club(E) 77-10
-2	Russian Ragout	Dawn Club(E) 77-10
-1	Sweet Georgia Brown	Dawn Club(E) 77-10

The original title of *Russian Ragout* was *Russian Rag & Blues*.

Art & Jan Hodes

Art Hodes, Jan Hodes, p duet.

Acton, London.   5 May 1988

In The Mood	unissued
After Hours	un-numbered private issue [cassette]
Chicago Medley	un-numbered private issue [cassette]
Watermelon Man	un-numbered private issue [cassette]
12th Street Rag	un-numbered private issue [cassette]
How Long Blues	un-numbered private issue [cassette]
Pinetop's Boogie Woogie	un-numbered private issue [cassette]
Caravan	un-numbered private issue [cassette]
Cow Cow Blues	un-numbered private issue [cassette]

Art Hodes, p solo.

Same session.

| I'm Gonna Sit Right Down & Write Myself | |
| A Letter | un-numbered private issue [cassette] |

Cambridge, England.   6 May 1988

| St. Louis Blues | un-numbered private issue [cassette] |

This un-numbered private issue was a 100-copy limited edition distributed to friends by Art & Jan Hodes.

Jim Galloway/Art Hodes

Jim Galloway, ss-1/bar-2; Art Hodes, p.

Café des Copains, Toronto, Ont.   25 September 1988

| I Would Do Most Anything -1 | Music & Arts CD610 [CD] |

Exactly Like You -1	Music & Arts CD610 [CD]
Some Of These Days -2	Music & Arts CD610 [CD]
Squeeze Me -1	Music & Arts CD610 [CD]
Doing The New Lowdown -1	Music & Arts CD610 [CD]
Tennessee Waltz -1	Music & Arts CD610 [CD]
Dear Old Southland -1	Music & Arts CD610 [CD]
If I Had You -1	Music & Arts CD610 [CD]
Just A Closer Walk With Thee -2	Music & Arts CD610 [CD]
Just A Little While To Stay Here -1	Music & Arts CD610 [CD]

Art Hodes, p solo.
   Same session.

The Preacher	Music & Arts CD610 [CD]
Tomorrow's Blues	Music & Arts CD610 [CD]

Wild Bill Davison — Art Hodes with John Petters Dixielanders

Wild Bill Davison, c; Jack Free, tb; Trevor Whiting, cl-1/ss-2/ts-3; Art Hodes, p; Keith Donald, sb; John Petters, d.
   Bull's Head, Barnes, London.   28 October 1988

My Monday Date -1	CMJ(E) MC003 [cassette]
Rocking Chair -1	CMJ(E) MC003 [cassette]
Am I Blue? -3	CMJ(E) MC003 [cassette]
Back In Your Own Backyard -2	CMJ(E) MC003 [cassette]
I've Got The World On A String -1	CMJ(E) MC003 [cassette]
I Never Knew -1, 2	CMJ(E) MC003 [cassette]
Limehouse Blues -1, 2	CMJ(E) MC003 [cassette]
Reunion Blues -3	CMJ(E) MC003 [cassette]
As Long As I Live -1, 2	CMJ(E) MC003 [cassette]

Trevor Whiting, ss; Art Hodes, p; Keith Donald, sb; John Petters, d.
   Same session.

Once In A While	CMJ(E) MC003 [cassette]

Trevor Whiting, ss; Art Hodes, p; John Petters, d.
   Same session.

Three Little Words	CMJ(E) MC003 [cassette]
Wrap Your Troubles In Dreams	CMJ unissued

Trevor Whiting's instrument is not confirmed on the unissued title.
Art Hodes, p. solo
   Same session.

Melancholy Blues	CMJ unissued

Trevor Whiting, ss; Art Hodes, p; John Petters, d.
   Bletchingly Jazz Circle, Bletchingly, Surrey, England.   3 November 1988

Blues In The Night	CMJ(E) MC003 [cassette]

Art Hodes, p. solo
   Same concert.

Grandpa's Spells	CMJ(E) MC003 [cassette]

Art Hodes

Art Hodes, p solo.
   ? London.   3 November 1988

unknown titles	Black Lion(E) unissued

London. 4 November 1988

Grandpa's Spells	Candid(G) CCD79037 [CD}
Mamie's Blues	Candid(G) CCD79037 [CD]
High Society	Candid(G) CCD79037 [CD]
Mr. Jelly Lord	Candid(G) CCD79037 [CD]
Buddy Bolden's Blues	Candid(G) CCD79037 [CD]
Pagin' Mr. Jelly	Candid(G) CCD79037 [CD]
Original Jelly Roll Blues	Candid(G) CCD79037 [CD]
Winin' Boy Blues	Candid(G) CCD79037 [CD]
Beale Street Blues	Candid(G) CCD79037 [CD]
Wolverine Blues	Candid(G) CCD79037 [CD]
Ballin' The Jack	Candid(G) CCD79037 [CD]
The Pearls	Candid(G) CCD79037 [CD]
Gone Jelly Blues	Candid(G) CCD79037 [CD]
Doctor Jazz	Candid(G) CCD79037 [CD]
Oh! Didn't He Ramble	Candid(G) CCD79037 [CD]

Art Hodes & Marcus Belgrave

Marcus Belgrave, t; Art Hodes, p.

Moot Court Auditorium, University of Windsor, Ont. 11 December 1988

Hot 'N Cool	Parkwood(Ca) PW113 [cassette]
Blue Monk	Parkwood(Ca) PW113 [cassette]
Creole Love Call	Parkwood(Ca) PW113 [cassette]

Index of Names

Books in the Series Music in American Life

Only a Miner: Studies in Recorded Coal-Mining Songs
Archie Green

Great Day Coming: Folk Music and the American Left
R. Serge Denisoff

John Philip Sousa: A Descriptive Catalog of His Works
Paul E. Bierley

The Hell-Bound Train: A Cowboy Songbook
Glenn Ohrlin

Oh, Didn't He Ramble: The Life Story of Lee Collins
as Told to Mary Collins
Frank J. Gillis and John W. Miner, Editors

American Labor Songs of the Nineteenth Century
Philip S. Foner

Stars of Country Music: Uncle Dave Macon to Johnny Rodriguez
Bill C. Malone and Judith McCulloh, Editors

Git Along, Little Dogies: Songs and Songmakers of the American West
John I. White

A Texas-Mexican *Cancionero*: Folksongs of the Lower Border
Americo Paredes

San Antonio Rose: The Life and Music of Bob Wills
Charles R. Townsend

Early Downhome Blues: A Musical and Cultural Analysis
Jeff Todd Titon

An Ives Celebration: Papers and Panels of the Charles Ives
Centennial Festival-Conference
H. Wiley Hitchcock and Vivian Perlis, Editors

Sinful Tunes and Spirituals: Black Folk Music to the Civil War
Dena J. Epstein

Secular Music in Colonial Annapolis: The Tuesday Club, 1745-56
John Barry Talley

Bibliographical Handbook of American Music
D. W. Krummel

Goin' to Kansas City
Nathan W. Pearson, Jr.

"Susanna," "Jeanie," and "The Old Folks at Home": The Songs of
Stephen C. Foster from His Time to Ours Second Edition
William W. Austin

Songprints: The Musical Experience of Five Shoshone Women
Judith Vander

"Happy in the Service of the Lord": Afro-American Gospel
Quartets in Memphis
Kip Lornell

Paul Hindemith in the United States
Luther Noss

"My Song Is My Weapon": People's Songs, American Communism,
and the Politics of Culture
Robbie Lieberman

Chosen Voices: The Story of the American Cantorate
Mark Slobin

THEODORE THOMAS: America's Conductor and Builder of Orchestras,
1835-1905
Ezra Schabas

"The Whorehouse Bells Were Ringing" and
Other Songs Cowboys Sing
Guy Logsdon

Crazeology: The Autobiography of a Chicago Jazzman
Bud Freeman, as Told to Robert Wolf

Discoursing Sweet Music: Town Bands and Community Life in
Turn-of-the-Century Pennsylvania
Kenneth Kreitner

Mormonism and Music: A History
Michael Hicks

Voices of the Jazz Age: Profiles of Eight Vintage Jazzmen
Chip Deffaa

Pickin' on Peachtree: A History of Country Music in Atlanta, Georgia
Wayne W. Daniel